MOUNTAINS OF THE W

de Teide 3720 m.
Camerún 4070 m.
Kilimanjaro 5895 m.
Kenya 5201 m.
Rás Daschan 4620 m.
Ruvenzori 5120 m.
Elbrus 5633 m.
Demavend 5465 m.
Everest 8848 m.
Godwin-Asten 8619 m.
Davalaghiri 8180 m.
Kinchinjunga 8480 m.
Kan-Tengri 7300 m.
Fujisama 3750 m.

AFRICA   ASIA

S. Elias 5489 m.
MacKinley 6194 m.
Hooker 4328 m.
Punta Blanca 4386 m.
de Sta. Marta 5300 m.
Fremont 4202 m.
Illimani 6405 m.
Aconcagua 6959 m.
Popocatepell 5452 m.
Sorata 6617 m.
Chimborazo 6267 m.
Huascarán 6768 m.
Orizaba 5550 m.

AMERICAS

Kosciusko 2240 m.
Cook 3768 m.
de Carlos Luis 5100 m.
Mauna Kea 4253 m.
de Aneto 3404 m.
Mulhacén 3478 m.
Blanco 4807 m.
Mus Alla 2936 m.
Tatra 2663 m.
Galdhopig 2560 m.
Urales 1689 m.

AUSTRALIA & POLYNESIA   EUROPE

Wine Routes of
ARGENTINA

OTHER BOOKS BY ALAN YOUNG

An Encounter With Wine
(Wine Information Bureau, Perth 1977)
new edition 1986

Australian Wines and Wineries
(Horwitz Grahame, Sydney 1983)

Australia-New Zealand Wine Year Book
(International Wine Academy 1986)

Making Sense of Wine -
A Study in Sensory Perception
(Greenhouse Publications, 1986)
new editions 1989, 1995

Making Sense of Wine Tasting
(Lennard Books, London 1987)

Chardonnay - The Definitive Guide
(Sidgwick & Jackson, London 1988)
new edition 1989
(International Wine Academy, 1991)
new edition 1994

Wine is Fun!
(International Wine Academy, 1995)
Chinese Edition 1997

Wine Routes of
ARGENTINA

Alan Young

Consulting Editor
Dereck H. N. Foster

INTERNATIONAL
WINE ACADEMY
SAN FRANCISCO
SYDNEY

First published in 1998 by

International Wine Academy

38 Portola Drive

San Francisco CA USA 94131

Fax: 1 415 641 7348

ayoung@sirius.com

3 Argyle Street, Camden,

NSW 2570 Australia

Copyright © 1998 by Alan Young

Cover design by Tony Cooper

Cover photo by Augusto Foix

Maps by Barry R. Nelson and Gary Chen

Set in 11.5pt Palatino

Library of Congess Catalogue Card

ISBN 0 9596983 2 9

Distributed in the USA by The Wine Appreciation Guild
1 800 231 9463

CONTENTS

DEDICATION

To my travelling companion, best friend
and supporter; all are my wife, Norma.

FOREWORD

MARQUES DE GRIÑON

DON CARLOS FALCÓ Y
FERNANDEZ DE
CÓRDOVA

Alan Young in *Wine Routes of Argentina* displays the key attributes of a wine writer
- a deep knowledge of viticultural practices, wines and winemakers from around
the world; complete independence and the ability to express the resulting array of
complex and often subjective information in direct, understandable prose. He also
dispels many pre-conceived notions, folklore, snobbery and romanticisms associated with this wonderful subject of wine and winemaking.

Wine Routes of Argentina is an ambitious and fascinating work. Argentina, the
world's fourth largest wine producer - after Italy, France and Spain - has remained
until very recently a sleeping giant. The author shows how the Argentine wine
industry has been unwilling to use, or is ignorant of, its huge potential in the
international markets.

My experience as a winemaker in Mendoza over recent vintages has been fascinating and rewarding. Expanding from my home bodega in Toledo, Spain, I am
now convinced that Argentina was the right place for me to start a New World
venture following the example of other leading European winemakers. Despite
Alan Young's understandable disdain for the viticultural abilities of my fellow
countrymen in the New World, the fact that they were the first to bring vines to
the Americas centuries ago reinforces my motivation to prove that great wines
can be made there.

For the fast growing world of winelovers, whether amateur or professional, Alan
Young's latest book provides an authoritative and attractive guide to a country
that will surely add, over the next few years, a new chapter to the amazing success
story of Southern Hemisphere wines.

I am sure that *Wine Routes of Argentina* will give the reader many hours of joy
and knowledge of this exciting country - and its wine industry.

ACKNOWLEDGMENTS

Writing a book is a difficult, engaging task. No person ever writes a book alone; the author is dependent on so many support people such as copy readers, designers, contributing friends and a whole host of technical support.

An international book requires friends who provide transportation, meals, accommodation, local knowledge, language translation, fellowship, and a belief in what you are doing.

This book started as a handout text for a class on South American wines given in San Francisco. At the seminar's end, I realized that I had more than half a book already completed. I thank those students for forcing me to compile the foundation material.

With one exception, the numerous trips to South America have been pleasurable tasks. It was on these journeys that a host of wonderful people all gave their hearts, tables and superb bottles. Outstanding amongst these wonderful people was Bs.As. chef Daniel Lopez Roca. New York wine authority, Norah Favelukas, was a power in the planning stages while at the other end of the Americas, Dr. Nicolas Catena enthused a group to make it all financially possible. Ing. Carlos Catania, of INTA research station and friend to all, never stopped contributing his enormous wealth of knowledge of Argentina wine regions, and personal friendship.

Almost everybody in the wine regions contributed unselfishly. Notable amongst these were the Ricardo Santos family of Mendoza, including wife Estela and son Patricio. Opera lovers Adriano Senetiner and Walter Brescia were gracious and generous hosts on numerous occasions

Thank you to everybody from my Bs. As. bodyguards, Jorge Avaca and Alejandro Romay, to those people who drove me back and forth to airports and bus stations in many parts of Argentina.

Following an incident that changed my life, the work was nearly abandoned. At that time numerous wonderful people came forward to get me back on track. No one contributed more to this than Dereck H.N. Foster, wine correspondent for *Buenos Aires Herald*.

At home in San Francisco, without the incredible computer program contribution and artistic design of Tony Cooper, and editing and journalistic support by Wendy Cooper, this work, without doubt would never have been satisfactorily concluded.

Surprisingly, accurate touring maps are not part of the Argentine wine scene. and Gary Chen spent countless hours correcting this anomoly.

From Patagonia to Salta there were many hundreds of others who contributed in some way or another — to you all, a giant thank you.

10

AUTHOR'S PREFACE

"You are too early with a book on Argentine wines, I made the same mistake with a book on Chilean wines 20 years ago". Sitting at a German wine industry lunch in a tent in Bordeaux, France, I thought how incongruous it was that a famous English author would be telling this to an Australian resident of the USA. Hugh Johnson, the world's most published wine writer in about 20 languages, is that sort of worldly, open person prepared to share his knowledge with all.

Yes, it probably is too early for a book on Argentine wines, yet a decade ago the very same Hugh Johnson said in one of his books that the world could no longer ignore the wines of Argentina.

Certainly, much progress has been made in Argentina since Johnson made this prophesy but, maybe, it still isn't time. Are they ready for helpful criticism?

With very few exceptions the Argentine wine industry is not ready for such a book and, in most cases, does not understand the need for such a book. As one person asked, "Why do you want to visit my winery?"

The only constant in the Argentina wine industry is change itself, very little is static. Perhaps this is the story to tell, the one of constant change.

The wines are changing dramatically with each vintage, but which wines do we write about in a book such as this? Are only the very best *talking* wines discussed, or, the everyday *drinking* wines?

Despite the valiant efforts of a precious few to reach the highest standards, most Argentine wines are destined, in the foreseeable future, to fill the places vacated successively by the French, Australian and Chilean $5-$8 wines. These are the everyday value-for-money, bang-for-your-buck, drinking wines. Argentina can do this well — and this category will dominate these pages.

It is an interesting story of many colors — dynamism, energy, apathy, extreme wealth, poverty, and a wonderful laid-back life style that does not belong in the 20th century, let alone the next one.

To the best of the writer's knowledge, Argentina is the only country in the world where harvesting operations shut down from Friday until Monday. The thought of visiting a winery on weekends is barely a consideration.

At the end of the 20th century, with very few exceptions, the future of Argentine wine quality is firmly in the hands of foreigners.

As in other countries the required technical knowledge, so necessary for quality wines, is still not available at home. This is an elastic gap, one that can be narrowed or widened at will; and, that is firmly in the hands of the Argentines.

11

The Inca capital of Cuzco, Peru, at 3,249 metres (11,000 feet) above sea level, is believed to be the origin of Argentina's grapes

HISTORY OF ARGENTINE WINES

Debate continues as to how, where and when the vine originally arrived in what is known today as Argentina. There are two valid theories. The first is that it came over the Andes from Chile, not an impossible feat when one considers that those arriving in Chile had many greater obstacles to overcome. Then, it was just a short walk over the 7,000 metre Andes!

Santiago (Chile) vine grower, Juan Jufré, in the late 1550s reportedly founded the Argentine city of San Juan. He is credited with helping to establish the vine in the tri-provinces of San Juan, San Luis and Mendoza. Mendoza was brought to life circa 1561 and historians say that vines were well established there by 1570. The northwest city of Santiago del Estero was Spain's first urban settlement in Argentina (1553) and keeps appearing as an original source of vines. Like Mendoza and San Juan, it was settled from Santiago del Chile.

The second theory has the vine traveling from Peru through Bolivia along the east side of the Andes via the Humahuaca Pass. If the Argentine vines did originate in Cuzco, south-eastern Peru, this is a logical story.

But the history of Argentine wine rests only lightly with the Spanish founders who were concerned mainly with plundering and raping the countries and cultures throughout North and South America. As in most of the southern cone countries, Peru, Bolivia, Brazil, Uruguay, it was the mass immigration from Europe, mainly Italy, in the mid-late 1800s that brought strength, vitality and versatility to Argentina.

At this time South America enjoyed unprecedented economic expansion but suffered miserably from under-population. Although Europe itself was suffering from famine, poverty and political instability, potential immigrants were fearful of the dreaded military and political turmoil in South America. Those wishing to emigrate had their eyes firmly fixed on the United States of America where land was cheap and industrialization was booming. Individual freedom was another powerful magnet.

Argentine lawmaker of the day, J.A. Alberdi, who fathered the constitution, believed it was government's role to foster European immigration. He envisioned Europeans occupying the vast empty spaces of his country with landowners, not farmhands. However, the Europeans had heard about the ferocity of the indigenous Indians and were not keen to travel abroad to lose their heads. Indians were rightly on the warpath until the late 1870s.

Also, an odd term, *Latifundism*, meaning large, open farms, discouraged European land ownership. Emigrants were also discouraged by the real lack of communication and problems of transpor-

13

tation in such a vast country. New arrivals had to overcome without - and then build all these facilities.

Despite these troubles, Argentina's population of 1.2 million doubled between 1857 and 1902 and by 1924 the population had increased to 10.25 millions. The productive rural area increased 60 fold and Argentina became the world's eighth richest country.

Italian emigrants accepted these challenges in Argentina, as they did in Brazil, Uruguay and faraway California. Fortunately, this strong Italian armada levelled the playing field and made Argentina a European, rather than a Spanish, culture. They also had a shattering effect on the local language. While they did not fulfill politician Alberdi's dream of settling the vast empty spaces, they certainly did take control in many places. Today, more than 50 percent of Argentina's people can trace their roots back to Italy.

The Italian legacy can be seen in many areas of the economy, most noticeably in retailing; particularly in the national capital Buenos Aires. Yet, it is their commitment to the oases, snug alongside the Andes, that is the flavor of this book.

The Republic of Argentina is a relatively young country, having secured independence from Spain on July 9, 1816. It became firmly established following the civil wars of 1860-61 when Buenos Aires became the seat of government. In 16th and 17th century days, much of the power was centred in the west and north western provinces of Tucuman, then Cordoba; with the strings being pulled by the Spanish viceroy in Peru. Mendoza and San Juan provinces had

their principal influence and links with Chile.

The *criolla de vino* or common vines that arrived in these regions were descendants and selections of the original vines that came from Spain via Mexico. Over a period of three centuries, the selections propagated in the newly established areas were hardy and heavy-bearing. They were the varieties *Mission* (Pais) for red wine and probably a *Muscat* (Moscatello) derivative for whites. For common everyday wines, these grapes were acceptable.

With the coming of the 19th century, winelover/settlers the New World over were looking for the wine styles and quality they had left at home. As ever, there were men to meet the challenge; the pattern having been set in Chile by Silvestre Ochagavia Echarazeta who imported the first *noble* varieties from Europe. Enter Miguel Aimé Pouget, a French technician who resided briefly in Chile. Before Pouget's arrival, a small research station (Quinta Normal) lacking in direction had been established in what is now downtown Mendoza. Pouget brought it very much to life

The Quinta became the centre of change. Noble varieties and French viticulture techniques that were working well in Chile were introduced. From all accounts, this was the first turning point towards quality oriented production.

The entrepreneurial Mendoza clone of Chile's Ochagavia and California's Haraszthy was the very bright 25 year old, Tiburcio Benegas who was born in Rosario. After arriving in Mendoza he succeeded in many fields, with a strong direction towards winegrowing, bank-

14

ing and politics. Benegas first established a workable bank while encouraging the building of the railway line from Buenos Aires to Mendoza.

Benegas married into a wine family and established a large vineyard/winery operation known as Trapiche. In 1970 the Benegas family sold Trapiche, South America's biggest wine operation today, to the Pulenta family (Peñaflor).

Prior to the railroad, western agricultural producers were not competitive in the main domestic markets because their goods required carriage by horse and cart for more than 1,000 kilometres (600 miles) to the populous suburbia of Argentina - and the ports for foreign markets. The British inspired railroads had one lasting effect in Mendoza - the establishment of the prestigious Norton winery in Lujan de Cuyo.

For the next (20th) century, Argentine winemakers had a captive and flourishing market and, apparently, all was well for many years. Then came a number of associated problems fired by political instability, the Dirty War, over-production, discounting and an economy rampant with inflation. Behind all this the Fascist military and church were pulling the strings of disaster.

Like Germany and Japan before them, it was not until a crushing defeat in the Falklands War that the Argentine people took back partial control of their country. Unlike the world's two economic super powers, Japan and Germany, the undoing of the military stranglehold was not complete. Along with the church the military still, not so unobtrusively, holds a powerful hand. These two powers, unheard of in today's Ja-

pan or Germany, will forever stifle the real wishes of Argentines.

Perhaps the Lonely Planet *Guide to Argentina* says it best: *Indeed, Argentina's inability to achieve its potential, despite its abundant natural resources, and its highly literate and sophisticated population, has mystified outside observers for decades. A country that, at the turn of the century, resembled now prosperous Australia and Canada has regressed instead of keeping pace with those countries.*

.....Argentina is one of Latin America's wealthiest countries, but its economy is in a perpetual state of chaos. To repay the crippling international debts would require all export earnings for 27 months. Mexico's foreign debt by contrast, equals only 13 months of that country's exports

And on the Church, the Guide says; *Like other Argentine institutions, the Church has many factions. During the late 1970s and early 1980s, the official Church generally supported the de facto military government despite persecution, kidnapping, torture and murder of religious workers.*

.....The Archbishop of Buenos Aires, for example, has defended President Menem's pardon of the convicted murderers and torturers of the Proceso, and it appears that official chaplains acquiesced in the atrocities of the Dirty War by counseling the perpetrators.

The son of a La Rioja winegrower, Carlos Saul Menem, himself a prisoner of the military, was given a Presidential mandate to right the wrongs of the past. There is no doubt that his administration has legislated reasonable fiscal reform albeit both brittle and fragile. The same story of crime and corruption rears its ugly head at almost every corner, but few people care. The bitter voice of personal experience has spoken!

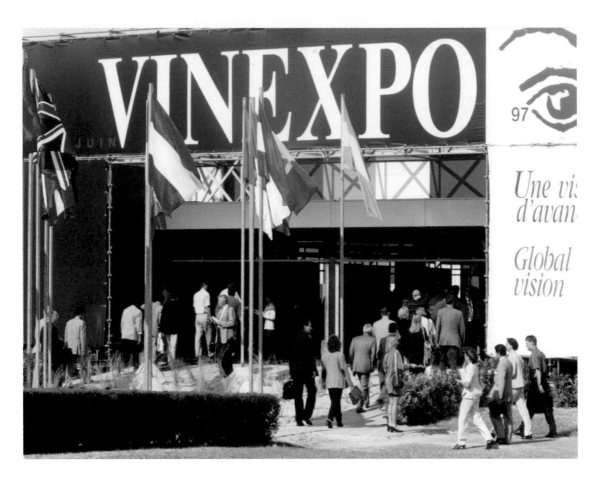

Vinexpo, one of the world's great wine exhibitions is held in Bordeaux, France, every odd year. Trade shows like this one are attended by wine buyers from around the world and offer Argentina the chance to show its wines to the trade during the week-long event.

THE 21ST CENTURY

Traditionally, Argentina with its strong Spanish and Italian heritage, has been a producer of bulk or common wines. The older generation consumed these wines at most meals without thought or posture — and consumption rocketed to 90 litres per head of population - man woman and child per year. This made Argentina the world's fourth most important wine consumer behind France, Italy and Spain.

A number of factors, including lifestyle and heavy promotion by the beer and soft drink industries between the 1980-90s, saw this figure plummet to less than half of its 1980 peak. Towards the end of the millennium, this 40 litres per head figure seems to have stabilized; one part of the good news.

The other part of the equation is that, consistent with an improved economy and wine quality, winelovers are paying considerably higher prices for their favorite beverage.

Varietal wines, made from a single grape variety grown in ideal locations, are now taking their place in the front rank of the world's wine.

Consciously or not, Argentina has chosen to have its own wine identity rather than being a French look-alike. The temptation to become yet another producer of the dreaded four - Cabernet, Chardonnay, Merlot and Sauvignon (blanc) - has been resisted in favor of their own specialties. Malbec is a remarkable red and Torrontes an arresting white when produced from the right vineyards and bodegas. And, these are not hard to find. These two flavorsome wines have already captured the imagination of winelovers around the globe.

This is not to say that the favored four are not produced in large quantity or quality - in Argentina they certainly are! All the way from Salta near the Bolivian border to the vast plains of Patagonia there are any number of eager producers waiting to pour these admirable wines. Still, the majority of Argentine wine producers desire to be accepted for their quality Malbecs rather than the other three popular Bordeaux varieties.

Despite a throbbing vein of hard work, there is much to be done in the vineyards. New technology is being readily accepted in some vineyards and wineries. Premium grape varieties are moving higher up the Andean foothills away from the security of the traditional furrow irrigation. These new heights demand expensive pump and sprinkler systems, a new experience for Argentine producers.

Experienced vineyard labor is becoming insufficient in many regions, labor is scarce, and will become more so in the two main provinces of Mendoza and San Juan. Already mechanical harvesters, although a rare sight, are at work, and this will forever change the industry. The traditional overhead *parral* trellising, the source of so much bulk wine, will have to go eventually, in favor of the more easily worked *espalier* trellises.

It has been heartening to observe this industry during this last decade when it moved from the darkest night to the dawning of a new tomorrow. Although a number of traditional bodegas produce a different style of wine, more than 95 percent of the 1,485 professional wineries registered with the National Institute of Vitiviniculture (INV), still produce what could rightly be called *old-fashioned* style wines. Some could be classified as 18th century wines.

A number of forward-looking producers are now making one style for the domestic and South American markets, and a more appealing international style for the export markets of Asia, Europe, North America and the Pacific countries. A smaller group have switched to only one style for all markets but these wines may come in different labels for each market.

The immediate future is both bright — and dim. On the bright side is a worldwide shortage of fine wines and many developing markets. This makes the task of breaking into global markets easier than a decade ago. Looking through the tunnel, the dim light for Argentine wine exports is marketing professionalism, a challenge that most producers still have to meet. The global market place is not easy; the competition is fierce.

On the other side of the coin, much can and should be done in the domestic market. Unfortunately, Buenos Aires, the biggest market, is at least 1,000 kilometres from the wine country that runs alongside the towering Andes. Only one third of this distance away is the thriving metropolis of Santiago, Chile and millions of Chileans who seek the yet unpolluted air, and wine, of Argentina; a market yet unexplored.

Throughout almost the entire wine world, wine and tourism go hand-in-hand, a lesson not generally understood by Argentine wine or tourism authorities. Oddly one must travel nearly 2,000 km from Bs.As. to Cafayate to find Bodegas Torino and Etchart who cater correctly for tourists. Trapiche, Norton, La Rural and Escorihuela are making a solid effort. Winelovers do like to explore wineries in foreign countries; just ask the Australians, Europeans, South Africans and North Americans!

Everything is in place for a sparkling future. There are many lessons to be learned from visiting and exhibiting in foreign countries and applying these lessons to the local scene. There is no question in this writer's mind that the best of Argentine wine can hold its own with the best of any other country.Now the challenge is, on the one hand, to elevate the overall industry standard — much can be done here. On the other hand, dedicated people are needed to produce great wines from the newer varieties planted in the right regions.

Let us raise our glasses to a long, healthy and happy future, for Argentina, and its winelovers!

UNDERSTANDING ARGENTINE NAMES

Similar to Washington, Lincoln and Main Streets in the USA, or George, William and Elizabeth in the British colonies, Argentine towns of all sizes have streets and suburbs that carry the names of, mainly, former liberators and generals. The odd admiral receives a rare mention. No one stands out like *the* Libertador himself, General José de San Martin, whose troops won Argentina's independence and also helped in Chile and Peru. In local situations, streets are sometimes named after the wife of a notary and, also, prominent locals such as doctors, artists and the like.

1536 Pedro de **Mendoza** financed an expedition to *Nuestra Señora Santa Maria del Buen Aire* which was a disaster. Indians overcame the attempt for a Spanish settlement at the site of the present day Buenos Aires. Mendoza died shortly after on the voyage back to Spain. Buenos Aires was resettled permanently in 1580. The city of Mendoza was named for the Governor of Chile, Sr. García H. de Mendoza.

Other stand-out names, events, and reputed achievements are:
25 de Mayo, (25 May) 1810, Ferdinand VII granted autonomous government to administer the Vice Royalty of Rio de la Plata (silver) i.e. Argentina, Paraguay and Uruguay
25 de Mayo, 1853 Constitution adopted for the entire nation
 9 de Julio, (9 July) 1816 Independence of the United Provinces of Rio de la Plata
 9 de Julio, 1862 Independence from Spain

Year elected President:
1826 Bernardino **Rivadavia** named President, resigned in one year due to failure to bring about dramatic changes. Rivadavia worked for a cultural revolution that would replace the Spanish-Catholic culture with a modern secular and scientific culture shaped by British, French and USA thinking. Unfortunately Rivadavia was replaced by, possibly, Argentina's most brutal President, Juan Manuael **de Rosas**. He represented the conservative reaction against Rivadavia's reforms.
1852 José de *Urquiza* defeated Rosas' troops. Rosas led a reign of terror for too many years.
1862 Gen. Bartolome *Mitre* was the first President of the Argentine nation.
1868 Domingo *Sarmiento,* a scholar and writer, became President.
1880 Gen. Julio Argentino *Roca* who lead the war against the indigenous southern Indians, was elected President.
1916 Hipolito **Yrigoyen** elected President
1946 Juan Domingo **Peron** elected President by popular poll.

19

HELPFUL SPANISH WORDS

Barrica	Wine barrel of 228 litres
Bodega	Winery (warehouse)
Bomba	Pump
Caramañola	Bocksbeutel (Rose) shaped bottle
Carretera/Ruta	Highway
Cerro	Hill or mountain
Chacra	Farm
Chicha	Partially fermented wine
Cooperativa	Co-operative winery
Corcho	Cork
Cordillera	Mountain range
Cosecha	Picking of the grapes
Cuba	Large fermentation vat
Cuyo	Sandy earth - Huarpe Indian word
Degustación	Tasting
Denomiación de Origen (DO)	Lujan de Cuyo, Maipu, San Rafael and La Rioja are official DOs, recognized regions.
Elaboración	Making and elevation of wine
Enologo	Enologist or winemaker
Estancia	Ranch
Etiqueta	Label
Finca/Fundo	Farm
Gerente	Manager - winery
Granizo	Hail
Ingeniero Agronomo	Agronomist - vineyard manager
Levadura	Yeast
Mosto	Grape juice - must - before fermentation
Poda	Pruning
Prensa	Wine press
Provincia	State
Puente	Bridge
Punta	Point
Racimo	Grape cluster
Riego	Irrigation
Roble	Oak
Uva	Grape berry
Vendimia	Time of the grape harvest
Vid	Vine
Viña	Wine company or vineyard
Viñedo	Vineyard
Vino	Wine

CLIMATE & WEATHER

Argentine geography changes from wide Atlantic Coast beaches to rugged summits, in the Andes. Stretching from 22° South for 3,000 kilometres (1,800 miles) to 55° South, its Northern Hemisphere equivalent would be from Cuba to Hudson Bay, Canada. Just west of Mendoza is Mt. Aconcagua at 7,021 metres (23,000 feet) the loftiest summit in the Western Hemisphere. Between these extremes can be found the vast humid pampas plains, rugged hills, desert plateaus and oases, glaciers, deep gorges and fertile valleys.

Much of Argentina is semi-arid to arid, and almost the entire country is subject to frosts. The principal wine producing province of Mendoza averages less than 200mm (8") of rainfall annually; still more than its neighboring provinces. This climate has a number of advantages, not the least being almost free from many diseases that require expensive spray programs for healthy grapes.

Climate and weather ultimately determine the composition of the grape berry, and this decides the quality of the wine. Understand this and you will understand wine.

It really is that simple; *wine is made in the vineyard*. Such diverse places as Greece, Mexico, Uruguay and the states of Texas and New Mexico (USA) are excellent examples of good winegrowing regions that produce world class wines.

Only in the English language is there a word for winemaker. In every other language the comparable word is wine grower, the emphasis being in the vineyard; not the winery.

It does not matter whether it is the world's most famous — or worst — grape growing region, good climate and weather make good grapes. What this means, in fact, is that almost undrinkable wines, say one or two points on a scale of ten, only, can be made in a year of bad weather — even in the most famous wine growing regions. Yet a 10/10 wine can be made in a year of ideal weather in what some consider an ordinary growing region. Argentina has many splendid regions for wine.

Climate is measured, or described, by the long term averages. Climate determines which grape varieties will grow best in a given region — or even a specific site within a vineyard. Climate will also dictate whether the grapes will ripen properly or not. *Weather is the day-to-day variation of those averages*. Weather helps to explain the particular characteristics of a given wine each year and why it may be different (better or worse) than the "standard" for that appellation. The best vintages occur when specific weather variables can be considered "normal".

There is another interesting subtlety about climate and weather. In many

21

parts of the world an *appellation* represents an opportunity to differentiate between *meso* and *macro* climates within one climate region. Mendoza, and on the other side of the world, Australia's Barossa Valley, have some similarities. The valley floors will ripen the grape varieties that require warm and long growing seasons e.g. the Cabernets, Sauvignon, Semillon and Syrah. The slopes of the peaks, which often carry snow, are admirable for the Burgundy and German varieties such as Chardonnay, the Pinots and Riesling. Unlike the Barossa, Mendoza is alongside the mighty Andes, with snow as the life-blood of the region.

Elements Of Weather

The elements of weather that affect vine development are: *temperature, humidity, rain, sunshine, cloud cover (fog), wind, frost, hail/thunderstorms, snow.*

Temperature. Winegrowing regions are classified as either *cold, cool, mild, warm, hot,* or *very hot*. Vines prefer cool to cold,wet winters - and warm to hot, dry summers. Grape vines need winters that are cool enough for the vine to have a dormant period. Vine-kill can result from winters that are too cold.

Soil temperature will affect the *microclimate* around the vine. Sandy soils respond quicker to spring warmth than clay soils. If a vigneron has both sandy and clay soils in a marginal growing area, varieties requiring the longest growing season are best planted on the sandy soil. This will create more rapid root and vegetative growth.

Many wine regions of the world have gravelly stones (large stones — not peb-

bly like Australian gravel). Some districts of Mendoza have much larger stony soil. These stones gather heat during the day which, when re-emitted during the cool evenings, has the effect of lengthening the growing day. Large bodies of water such as lakes and rivers have a similar *mesa*-climate effect. Many of the great wine regions are close to a flowing river or lake.

Heat Summation. In an endeavor to classify temperatures within wine-growing regions, during 1944 researchers at the University of California, Davis (UCD), renewed a system developed in 1735, which has been refined over the ensuing centuries.

Researchers in Australia and New Zealand have spent many years improving the UCD system because of an inherent weakness in measuring the cold and cool climates. They have devised an effective *Latitude Temperature Index* (LTI) (Jackson & Cherry 1988). The LTI focuses on cold-cool climates in both hemispheres because of their longer daylight hours — and the subsequent ability to photosynthesize at a rate greater than that proposed in other heat summation systems.

Australian scientist, JTO Kirk, has proposed an updated UCD system based on six, rather than five categories to remove the blurring between cool and warm by adding a *mild* category.

A cold region, such as Cork, Ireland, is best described as one where grapes will *not* ripen in some seasons. A cool region such as Lake Erie, USA, is one in which grapes are grown in the coolest possible region in which they will *consistently* ripen. Rio Negro is such a region.

Each grape variety has its own length of growing period. Some can ripen in 90 days, others require 200 days or more. In the southern hemisphere some varieties ripen in February, others in April, May, or even June. For this reason, only certain varieties will ripen in cold climates. Among the popular premium varieties, (Gewurz) Traminer, Chardonnay and the three Pinots - *blanc, gris, noir* - have short growing seasons, ripen early and are normally at their best when grown in the most southern (or northern) climates.

Most black grapes for red wine require a longer growing season and will not ripen in cold climates *i.e.* short summers.

Humidity is responsible for much of the disease occurring in grape vines on the east coast of all continents, but is not necessarily restricted to coastal regions.

The east coasts of Argentina, Uruguay, Brazil, China, Japan, Australia and the USA are all humid and growers must spray continually (almost weekly) during the growing season to control downy mildew and botrytis/bunch rot. West coast growers on these continents may spray as little as three times annually for these problems.

Precipitation/rain:

Too much:

• at flowering will reduce the number of berries per bunch
• during the growing year will necessitate costly spray programs to control rot and mildew
• at harvest time will cause berry splitting and bunch rot, lower sugars and acids
• creates problems moving equipment

in the vineyard.

Too little rain causes:

• small shoots and low leaf area.
• reduces quantity of juice (concentration); will increase skin thickness
• adds more color and tannin

To make commercial viticulture work in Argentina's desert-type climate it was necessary to build massive irrigation systems including dams and underground wells (bores) of which there are now over 30,000 in use for grape growing. The Incas, who ranged all along the Andes, have never been given credit for their incredible understanding of hydraulic engineering. They created the pattern for modern-day irrigation in the Cuyo which was then refined by the Huarpe Indians. Pioneer surveyor, A. Cipolletti, was the local who fine-tuned their work for today's needs.

Sunshine: Note that temperature and sunshine, while related, are different elements in the vineyard. The hours of sunshine during the growing season increase as we move away from the equator — north or south. This makes it possible to ripen grapes in France's northern area of Champagne or the Rio Negro in the south, even though the climate is relatively cold.

Hours of sunshine vary enormously within any given country, regardless of size. Sunshine is essential for the proper physiological maturation of wine grapes. Too much sunshine can also be a major problem at almost every stage of grape development.

At flowering, sun can cause *shatter* (chicken and egg). Rather than *setting* on the bunch, many potential berries fall to the ground. Shatter can also be caused

23

by too much cold weather. Later in the season, cooked berries result from persistent hot weather, giving the finished wine an unpleasant flavor.

Cloud/fog: When sunshine is manipulated by cloud and fog, it moderates the climate allowing cool climate grape varieties to grow in an otherwise hot climate. Fog is cloud in contact with the ground.

Wind: Wind can play both good and bad roles. Strong winds are normally a negative force because they break tender growing shoots. Following any form of precipitation, wind can be a favorable ally in removing residual moisture from the leaves and grape bunches, thus avoiding bunch rot.

Where hot and strong winds are a regular summer feature, they will create water stress and other problems on vine physiology, particularly in closing down the plant's stomata. These tiny pores are necessary to allow entry of CO_2 for photosynthesis. Argentina's *Zonda* hot wind can cause havoc at flowering time and might reduce crops by half. No air movement at all presents another problem, by allowing heat build up within the vine canopy. A gentle breeze will refresh the micro climate and allow healthy plant respiration.

Frost: Because spring frosts are an annual threat to many winegrowers the world over, sitings of new vineyards are carefully planned to avoid frost "pockets". Rio Negro can be subjected to severe frosts at the most unexpected times. Long established vineyards in frost prone areas have developed many methods in an attempt to combat this menace which devastates vines in much

the same way as does fire. Air propellers, overhead sprinklers, gas fires, oil pots and even helicopters are some of the standard protection methods.

The compound grape bud has three buds and under normal conditions only the primary bud will grow. If the primary bud is destroyed (e.g. burnt by frost) all is not lost. The secondary bud, and even the tertiary bud, will grow. The secondary bud will provide a crop, al-

Mid-season frost damage, General Roca

beit only about one third of the normal crop. The tertiary bud is unlikely to produce fruit.

Autumn frosts can kill leaves and stop fruit from ripening. Yet, under normal conditions, some marvellous *ice* wines are the products of mid-winter in Austria, Canada and Germany.

Hail: Coming mainly in the spring and early summer as a result of thunderstorms, hail to the vinegrower is the most savage of all weather elements. Hail shreds the leaves and fruit of the current crop. Yet, the biggest damage is the devastation of the next season's buds which will greatly reduce the following year's crop. Hail is a big problem in many regions of Argentina and the South Island of New Zealand.

Extremes: Like the human body, vines do not enjoy extremes of food, water or temperature. An unbalanced diet of any of these factors will reflect in the berry juice; this in turn will reflect in wine quality. Stress is an oft spoken, dangerous and relative term which should be used with extreme caution. It has a very

Hail-damaged canes above netting.

different connotation in the New World as opposed to the limited stress known in Europe. Insufficient water retards growth; too much water will either cause over-cropping and reduced fruit quality, or water-log the roots and deprive them of oxygen.

Excessive heat will close down the vine and stop it functioning; this plays havoc with the chemical balance of the berry. Insufficient heat will create unfavorable conditions for ripening. Many a year, in many a region, grapes can be seen hanging on the vines waiting for the last rays of summer sunshine to ripen the fruit - and often the sunshine fails to come.

Climatic regions explained. Climate can vary within one single vineyard, let alone within a village, district or county. For this reason, climates have been defined (Smart 1984) into three categories:

micro-climate, meaning the area (metres) around a plant or canopy;

meso-climate, or site climate, meaning the larger area (hundreds of metres) embracing the whole vineyard and associated regions of similar climate, but differentiated by elevation, slope, aspect, or proximity to a large body of water;

macro-climate, meaning regional climate as determined by a central weather recording station.

Classification of Growing Regions

Marine west coast (MWC). The normal MWC climate expects rain to fall during each of the 12 months. Marine west coast climate produces wines lower in alcohol and body than warmer areas, yet they are distinguished by intense varietal character and aroma.

MWC climate will not grow the warmth loving varieties of France and Italy. MWC is more suited to the Pinots and the German varieties, especially the more recent vinifera hybrids, such as Reichensteiner, Ehrenfelser and Optima.

Mediterranean climate: Mediterranean climate has winter rains and warm-hot summers. As the name implies, this type of climate is that known to the countries facing the Mediterranean: Spain, France and Italy. Some regions of California, Australia, Chile and South Africa share

25

white wine from white grapes. Of course, "white" grapes and wines aren't really white, but varying degrees of yellow and green.

The size of the grape berries can be indicative of wine quality. As an example, some of the best varieties such as Traminer, Cabernet Sauvignon, Riesling and Pinot noir have small berries on small clusters. Also, there are several distinctive berry shapes; however, no relationship between berry shape and wine quality has been suggested to date.

Grape clusters or bunches are described as *loose, well-filled* or *compact*. These differences can become quite important when the weather turns bad before harvest - tight clusters being far more susceptible to mildew and rot than loose, easy drying clusters.

A few hundred varieties are cultivated for winemaking, their origins being a study in geography. Over the centuries each of the main winegrowing regions in Europe recognized the different varieties that had been left by the conquerors, keeping only the few which grew best in their own district.

Thus, French Burgundians limit themselves to Pinot noir, Chardonnay, Gamay, Aligote and little else. Growers in the Rhone River regions have come to prefer Syrah, Grenache, Carignane, Roussane and Marsanne. By contrast, the growers of Bordeaux in SW France favor Merlot, the Cabernet varieties and their close relatives, both red and white.

German winemakers specialize in Riesling, Muller-Thurgau, Scheurebe and other varieties which are suited to their climatic conditions. Italians and Spanish have their own excellent varieties but outside of Barbera, Sangiovese (Italian), and Grenache (Garnacha) of Spain, little is seen of these grapes in the New World.

No Southern Hemisphere country has indigenous vines as did the Americas, Europe and northern Africa. The first Australian vines were gathered on opposite sides of the world -- the Cape of Good Hope, Rio de Janiero and from collections in Europe. South African import of vines goes back to the 16th century

Unlike the freedom enjoyed by New World winegrowers in choosing viticultural lands, European growers have government controls over where they can plant vines and which varieties can be planted. This allegedly protects the existing "personality" of a region, but tends to inhibit the development of new and improved varieties there. Argentine winegrowers do not have these restrictions - yet. The move towards *denominación de origin* will make Argentines think carefully about what should be planted and where. Without doubt, this will be good for everyone.

WHITE WINE GRAPES

Chardonnay: Small-medium, round berries, well-filled clusters, early ripening.

Chardonnay is the source of excellent white wines grown in many countries, as well as sparkling and table wines the world over. It exhibits a wide climatic tolerance and can produce impressive quality when grown in almost any climatic region.

The vine is vigorous and easy to farm except for a susceptibility to mildew and botrytis. Because the buds push out early in spring, Chardonnay vines are subject to frost damage.

Formerly limited to 6 to 7 tons per hectare, yields in many areas have doubled in the past decade due to the use of newer clonal selections. Chardonnay is a good performer in all Argentine regions, I believe best when grown in Agrelo and Tupungato.

Chenin (blanc): Medium-large, oval berries, compact clusters, mid-season ripening.

Grown in the right regions, Chenin can be a truly wonderful variety, even carrying modest amounts of barrel fermentation and ageing to advantage.When grown in irrigated, warm-hot climates on good soils, the yield can be as high as 25 to 30 tons per hectare. Clusters are winged or even double, conical and compact. Berries are juicy and tough-skinned. The fruit is subject to rot, especially when over-cropped in humid conditions.

Chenin maintains good acidity with good flavor in hot areas. It is considered a good blending variety, the flavor being compatible with a large number of more distinctive varieties, from Chardonnay to Semillon. For Argentina, Chenin is a grape of the future.

Pinot gris: Small, round berries; small, compact clusters, early.

Some would say that this is truly the world's best white (*gris*=grey) wine, albeit undiscovered except for Alsace, France and Kaiserstuhl, across the river in Germany. Almost a blue colored grape, it has all the same problems of the Pinot family such as compact bunches which are problematic in wet years. Pinot gris can be barrel fermented and aged for intense complexity. It is known as Pinot Grigio in Italy. Will do well in Argentina's cool climates: Agrelo, Uco Valley and Rio Negro.

Riesling: Small clusters, round berries, compact, mid-season.

Fruit is susceptible to sunburn which can cause skin and juice browning and destroy the varietal flavor. Light pinkish portions appear on exposed sides of many clusters.

In cold and cool vineyard regions, this variety produces delicate, flowery and perfumed wines of great distinction. Has great promise in Uco Valley and Rio Negro.

Sauvignon (blanc): Small-medium, oval berries, compact clusters, early ripening

New Zealand, where the varietal flavor is at its most emphatic levels, is probably the world leader in this variety. The flavor is intense and in cool climates it becomes minty or lime-like.

Skins are thin and the variety is easily susceptible to *botrytis cinerea,* or noble rot; even when humidity isn't high. As yet, the right regions and clones have not been found in South America for this variety, despite a lot of noise from Chile.

Semillon: Medium-large, round berries, compact clusters, mid-season ripening.

Following successful centuries as a dessert wine, Semillon is used increasingly for dry white table wines.

The berries are thin-skinned and juicy with a definite yellow color and many flavor layers peculiar to each region. The thin skins are susceptible to mould infections. In cool climates, the normal melon or fig-like flavor becomes distinctly grassy. Semillon table wine, if good to start with, can age beautifully in the bottle for 10 years or even longer. Another white variety that should find a home amongst Argentina's best wines.

Traminer (Gewurz): Small oval berries & clusters, compact.

One of the earliest ripening of all varieties, this Italian grape from the village of Tramin, Bolzano, is at its best in cool climates. A spicy variant *Gewurz*traminer is grown widely, but not all Traminer grapes are spicy. It is often planted in medium-warm regions, presumably because of its unusually "spicy, flowery" flavor. In warm climates Traminer wine tends to be low in acid with high pH. However, under the right growing conditions, the variety produces memorable sweet wines.

Although considered a white grape, Traminer fruit is noticeably pink in color. Skins are tough and yields are moderate. This wine is an ideal accompaniment to many Chinese dishes.

RED/BLACK GRAPES

Cabernet Sauvignon: Small, round berries, loose clusters, ripens late season.

Some claim this is the only grape allowed in Heaven! Its wines are known for pronounced flavor, color, body, acidity and longevity. Sadly, the media-driven Cabernet fervor has caused many winelovers to overlook a number of equally pleasurable wines of exquisite flavor such as Barbera, Malbec, Nebbiolo, Pinot noir, Sangiovese, Syrah, Tempranillo and Zinfandel.

The tough skin and loose cluster help make this grape very resistant to mildew, bunch rot, botrytis and other diseases. The Cabernets are also winemakers wines, fermenting smoothly, handling well and ageing well in wood and in bottle.

Cabernet Franc: Small, round berries, loose clusters, late.

A close relative of Cabernet Sauvignon, this variety is also a Bordeaux native. It is often blended with Merlot and Cabernet Sauvignon in many areas to produce good red wines.

The varietal aroma is intense, reminiscent of raspberries and, sometimes, violets. Similar to Cabernet Sauvignon in growth habits and ease of handling, the vigor is good and the yields are productive. However, it is more sensitive than Cabernet Sauvignon to mildew. I wish Argentina would forget about both Cabernets.

Cinsaut: Medium-large round berries, ripens mid-season.

Cinsaut is of interest mainly due to increased plantings in the French Mediterranean (50,000 hectares in production). It is sensitive to mildew and botrytis but does well in dry climates. Cinsaut fruit has good color and high acidity, a major bonus in hot climates. Its thick skin helps protect against disease and has a very definite future in the warmer climates of Argentina.

Grenache: Medium round berries, compact clusters, late-season.

Of Spanish origin, "Garnarcha" is the most prolific wine grape of Spain and an important variety in southern France, Australia and the central valley of California. It is used in the roses of Tavel and Lirac, the reds of Chateauneuf-du-Pape and Rioja (Spain) and in dessert wines of Banyuls in southeastern France.

A late maturing variety with heavy yields, it usually requires warm to hot climates for complete ripening. When grown in cool climates with reduced crop yields, Grenache wines exhibit an

intense strawberry-like aroma. Should be in the Argentine quality wine portfolio of the future.

Malbec (Cot): Small-medium, round berries, loose clusters, ripens mid-season.

Malbec is blended with Cabernet Sauvignon and Merlot in many countries - and with Carignane in some Mediterranean areas. Its use is generally to add softness and early maturity to the blend. In Australia, Malbec has been blended with Cabernet Sauvignon for many years and also used alone as a varietal. Definitely Argentina's red grape flag-bearer.

The wines of dark color, can be high in tannin, yet show a fruity softness, fruitiness and distinctive varietal character. Until recent clonal selections, Malbec suffered from poor fruit set, making it unappealing to growers elsewhere. Argentina's Malbec varietal wines can be sensational, mouth-filling wines.

Merlot: Small, round berries, loose clusters, ripens mid-season.

By far the most widely planted variety in Bordeaux, France, Merlot produces soft, perfumed wines which are often blended with Cabernet in many New World countries. It is one of the few European vines to succeed in Japan. South America has plantings in Argentina, Brazil and Chile.

All Bordeaux varieties appear to do best in a maritime influenced climate. Carefully selected clones may have a promising future in several Argentine wine areas; this all depends on carefully chosen clones.

Mourvedre (Mataro)*:* Small-medium, round berries, compact clusters, ripens late season.

Of Spanish origin, this wine yields moderately, produces deeply colored, alcoholic and robust wines that are normally used for blending. It produces good dry red table wines and port in Australia. Budburst is late in spring, an advantage in frost-prone areas. However, the late harvest is a disadvantage because of autumn rains. Grown well and wisely handled, Mouvedre is a variety with good potential in many Argentine wine regions.

Pinot noir: Small, round berries, compact clusters, ripens early.

When intelligently made in the right climatic years, Pinot noir, arguably, reaches heights not attained by other varieties. Aptly called a "minx", Pinot noir makes the highest classification of red wines in Burgundy as well as *methode traditionalle* sparkling wines right around the world. It is most suited to cool climates and is extensively planted in Switzerland, northern Italy and even Germany. Pinot noir is demanding for the viticulturist and many consider it difficult in the cellar. Compact bunches and thin skins make it vulnerable to almost any vineyard disease. It is an enormous challenge for Argentina's growers to produce a world-class wine. Pinot noir is a passionate love affair!

Syrah: Medium, oval berries, compact bunch, mid-late season.

Called both Shiraz and Hermitage in Australia, this Rhone variety produces a robust wine with ample color, fruit and tannin. Syrah is blended with as many as a dozen other varieties to produce the wines of Chateauneuf-du-Pape in France. Indications are that Syrah, following Malbec, will be a truly great Argentine wine, with classic varietal flavor and smooth as silk.

The best Syrah wines are made from low yielding vineyards while over-cropping will drastically reduce wine quality. The variety responds strongly to the climate of the growing region; wine quality may vary markedly from one vineyard to another.

Tempranillo: Medium-sized, compact clusters, ripens very early.

One day when the media critics overcome their mania for varietal wines they will realize the value in blending wines from different regions and grape varieties. Then the northern Spanish Tempranillo will be a variety of note. Becoming a real star in Portugal's booming Alentejo region where it is known as Aragonez, Tempranillo, a naturally low alcohol grape blends incredibly well with other Spanish varieties like Garnarcha and Graciano. Some of the better known Spanish exporters also blend with Bordeuax varieties, notably Cabernet Sauvignon. Already the Marquis de Griñon has made excellent indicator wines at Norton in Perdriel under the Duarte label.

Zinfandel: Medium, round berries, well-filled , ripens mid-late.

Almost nonexistent elsewhere, more than 12,000 hectares are planted to Zinfandel in California. Origin unknown although ampelographic (study of grapes) evidence traces it to the Primitivo variety of Italy's Apulia region.

In California, Zinfandel occupies the same workhorse role as does Syrah in Australia producing big volumes of light to full-bodied reds, excellent roses, occasional ports. Another variety with huge potential in the Lujan de Cuyo - Medrano areas, and possibly, San Rafael and cooler regions of San Juan province.

TASTEFUL TORRONTÉS

One of the world's most important wine competitions is conducted annually in London, UK by a prominent wine magazine. This event attracts thousands of entries and hundreds of judges from most wine producing countries. To reach the final trophy stage, a wine will have been judged at least six times.

It is hard to imagine the disbelief that overcame wine pundits in 1994 when an Argentine *Torrontés* was named as the Best White Wine. Most people had some idea where Argentina was located, but Torrontés had most observers baffled. "Where does it come from, what is it all about?" could be heard around the globe. There are many answers to this question; none would hold water, or wine.

Some say it is the Malvasia of Spain's Rioja region. There is a relatively poor Spanish variety known as Torrontés, but this is not the same vine. As usual, others say many unimportant things, none of which have any ampelographic credibility. Obviously it is a clone of something; we know not what yet. Who cares anyhow, it's marvellous!

In Argentina there are three distinct clones of Torrontés, all named after provinces - *Riojana, Sanjuanino* and *Mendocino*. While the province of La Rioja, and the department of Chilecito in particular, seems to be the epicenter of Torrontés, there is no question that it shines brightest in the more northern climes of Cafayate, Salta province. However there are many fine Argentine producers, Rio Negro has claims for a specially delicate Torrontés.

Barely below the Tropic of Capricorn at latitude 25.15°S, Salta compensates for its hot climate with some of the most striking high level scenes in the Mountains, if not the world. Several Torrontés vineyards are located at heights of more than 1900 metres (6400-6745 feet) above sea level. Here one can find the ultimate expression of an intensely aromatic and fruity wine, even at crop levels of 20-30 tonnes/ha. Not unlike a combination of the Muscat family including Gerwurztraminer, Torrontés is even more full-flavored and flowery. People love Torrontés because it tastes like wine, a bowl of fresh fruit and a bunch of flowers.

The La Rioja Co-operative, Chilecito, has gone one step further by producing Torrontés champagne, or sparkling wine. Now, that is different - and, a mouthful of wine! The Mendocino clone produces up to a high 50 tonnes/ha and is often used as a blending wine to elevate the flavor of lesser varieties.

One thing is certain about this normally dry, but seemingly sweet wine. Many believe that Torrontés is best consumed in its youth - more so in its first year.

MALBEC MAGIC !

"There is nothing quite like an Argentine Malbec wine," is an oft quoted phrase by the aficionado. Undoubtedly, it is Argentina's vinous signature wine, and this writer must confess to being terribly biased in its favor.

Unfortunately, media hype has placed Cabernet on a pedestal. This leads the tyro to believe that it is a "must-drink," thus depriving the eager winelover of the adventurous spirit to try other superb varieties such as Grenache, Malbec, Mouvedre, Nebbiolo; Syrah, Sangiovese or Pinot noir.

Unlike Cabernet Sauvignon, Malbec, or *Cot* as it is widely known, is a soft, generous wine. In fact, its primary role in its native Bordeaux, SW France is to soften and fill-out the savage Cabernet monster in its early years. Despite its almost universal acceptance in the region, it is the poor relation in the Medoc. Yet, over the river in Bourg-Blaye, where it is given the strange name *Auxerrois*, Malbec is a real star. Many a wine lover will tell you that Malbec is at its French best further east in the Cahors region. The writer's own experiences in Cahors would indicate that the Argentines are doing it better.

Malbec with 15,000 hectares (37,000 acres) is, by far, the most widely planted premium grape variety in Argentina. Locals will tell that it does well in many provinces. Keen observers say the variety is best when grown in the half-moon shaped area embracing Lujan, along the shallow clay and stony soils of the Mendoza River towards Medrano. The best wines come from old vineyards, some more than 70 years old, that produce small concentrated berries. As straight varietal wines, these are rich and complex with flavors of black cherries and blackberry. A very definite chocolate flavor can be found in the best wines.

Blends with Merlot and Cabernet can be found in many Argentine wineries; fortunately the Malbec tends to dominate the flavor of these wines.

Traditionally, Malbec has been grown close to the ground with old fashioned Guyot trellising. For the more technically inclined, modern techniques have found that, due to its natural upright growth, when trained onto higher espalier trellises, the vine and wine flavor respond well to vertical shoot positioning.

In the winery, fully-ripened Malbec has flavor to spare. It is equally enjoyable whether processed with or without oak barrel maturation; the wine certainly does not need any oak flavor for maximum enjoyment. Yet when aged in a mix of old and new, American and French oak barrels, it can provide another dimension for lovers of this wine style. Please make my red wine a Malbec!

PHYLLOXERA

In a sense, Argentine viticulture is sitting on a time bomb. In the worldly travels of the Vitis *vinifera* grapevine, a number of things went wrong, most of them due to an insect invisible to the naked eye, known as *phylloxera vasatrix*.

During the colonial days there were attempts to introduce vinifera vines into the settlements of eastern North America. In fact, an early US president, Thomas Jefferson, who collected French Bordeaux wines became interested in viticulture. He decided to obtain cuttings from France and tried to grow them in his Virginia garden. They started well but soon withered-up and died. At the time the reason for this failure was not known, but it foreshadowed the greatest disaster the international wine industry was to know. Next to Jefferson's ailing vinifera vines were some American *native* vines which grew without problems, producing ample crops of good fruit. Because of a "foxy" flavor, it was not liked for winemaking.

It wasn't until the mid 1800s that this same problem began to show in Europe, and when it did arrive it spread rapidly. The problem was the root-sucking aphid. It belongs in North America where the native vines and the insect co-exist in complete harmony.

Plant lovers and breeders are curious people. Some brought these interesting American vines back to Europe to hundreds of thousands of hectares of grapes that never had to co-evolve with phylloxera, had never developed a resistance to them. The European native plants had no way to defend themselves against this root-sucking louse.

Phylloxera spread like wildfire, turning the most valuable vineyards into cow farms. Firstly it went right through Europe and then to most other wine producing countries; South Africa Australia, New Zealand, Argentina and California; Chile was the single exception. And it was phylloxera that killed Thomas Jefferson's vines. A century and a half later many of the world's finest vineyards are again in big trouble.

During the later part of the 19th century, all over the world, all types of nonsensical legislation and quack cures were introduced in an endeavor to overcome this international vinous disaster.

The final solution came from an understanding of nature at work rather than from any of the crazy notions. If the American species were resistant to phylloxera why not use these roots and graft the vinifera scion to them? After all, these plants are compatible. During the early 1870s two French researchers named Viala and Revez gathered many of the American Vitis species and exposed them to phylloxera with the object of giving them a resistance rating. From these ratings three American native vines: V. berlandieri, V. riparia and V. rupesteris became the cornerstones of rootstocks the world over.

Ultimately, the rootstocks were planted throughout Europe and the rest of the world and onto these rootstocks were grafted the vinifera varieties such as the Pinots, Syrah, Chardonnay, the Cabernets, and so on. As ever, not all was well. Some growers could not give up old habits and crosses were made that included the vinifera species — a dumb decision. These became known as AXR #1 - 9. They were tested in several countries and failed miserably; phylloxera loved the vinifera parentage.

The main damage done by phylloxera occurs underground where the insects feed on the root tissue. In doing so they take away the contents of the cells, eventually killing the roots. Next they move onto more healthy roots for another destruction job. In California, where it is relatively dry, underground is only part of the cycle. However, some of these undergroundlings do surface as crawlers which obviously crawl to the next vine, or, are windblown. As such, they can adhere to a person's clothes, or machinery, and be transported to an unaffected vineyard where they setup another infestation.

Because of the ability to fly and the sexual nature, there are now new types, or bio-types. These have the ability to feed on various types of grapevines.

Whereas the AXR rootstock with its vinifera parentage didn't live for a minute in Europe, it survived in California until recently when a new phylloxera bio-type found its way to the west coast vineyards. This new bio-type has caused havoc with the predominately AXR rootstocks, causing the loss of hundreds of millions of dollars in vineyards.

Rootstocks can be resistant or tolerant towards the different diseases and pests that attack vines. The resistant vines have no appeal to the predators, whereas the tolerant ones co-exist with the problems. The insects can feed on the roots of resistant plants without affecting the vines productivity.

It is said that every ill wind blows some good. And, certainly, phylloxera did blow some good when California vineyards were replanted during the 1980s and '90s. Almost every vineyard replanted has many innovations such as different trellises, training systems, varieties and planting distances between vines and rows which yield better grapes. Without the need to replant, this would never have happened. Very few growers reverted to old systems.

Phylloxera has been in Argentine vineyards for many years but the continual dampness of furrow/flood irrigation has kept the pest inactive. When in 1955 the brothers Enrique and Pedro Zuloaga came to the Institute of Wine in Chacras de Corio, they commenced research on American rootstocks and developed a number of new grafting techniques.

As soon as irrigation is restricted with the intention of elevating grape quality, the phylloxera population increases noticeably. New vineyards being planted on higher hillsides, requiring drip or overhead irrigation, are very susceptible to infestation and the vines require tolerant rootstocks. The problem is the constant need for very careful monitoring — by people with much experience.

39

WINE STYLES

Are Argentine wines different to other wines, one might ask? Positively, yes! Better - no; worse - no; they are different. A second question might be - why?

All things being equal, wine quality and style, wherever the grapes may be grown, are dependent on the weather of that growing season. This is fully explained on pages 21-28. The vineyards of Argentina are located in a desert and cuddled up to the awesome Andes. The climate and weather are very different to any other place on earth. The climate here is *continental* desert. This favors grape varieties from a similar continental climate such as in the French Rhone region, and Italy's Piedmont and Chianti regions.

Two climatic examples, neighbors Chile and Brazil, are at opposite ends of the spectrum. Chile has a maritime *Mediterranean* climate which favors grapes from alike regions such as France's Bordeaux.

Brazil, and eastern Argentina for that matter, are very different, having an *east coast* humid climate. Different climates are the engines that drive wine *styles*, until the Joker, Man, gets his hand on the grapes. Wine can be no better than the grapes from which it is made.

But the Joker can alter the style by earlier grape picking with more acid, less sugar and flavor as is the case with champagne. Over-ripe grapes will give lots of flavor, more sugar, alcohol and less acid. These complex harvesting decisions will change the *style* and *structure* of the wine; but not the quality. That is locked in the grapes.

Due to massive domestic consumption, wine styles have been made for local appreciation - and that means with food; *e.g.* Pampas beef. Acid, which gives wine life, (peculiar to wine among all alcoholic beverages) is not liked by domestic consumers. In fact, most wine in the Mother countries of Italy and Spain are also traditionally low in acidity. Much of this is due to over-cropping.

The official classification of this wine is *mesa* or *table* wine. While there were, and still are, other classes such as *fino* and *reserva* these represent only a minute, but increasing fraction of production.

Three issues of varying importance changed Argentine wine styles. The primary issue was the re-birth of elected government at the end of military dictatorship in 1983. The new regime opted for free trade, opening Argentina to the world, and the world to Argentine goods. This meant competition, and Argentine winemakers unused to this trading situation, were ill-prepared for a full frontal blast.

Secondly, during the 1970s, a number of foreign companies, principally from France's Champagne region, brought their money and skills to Mendoza. While they did set new standards, none have approached the high quality they left behind in France.

40

The third issue was that of one man who visited California in 1976 and went home determined that Argentina could, and would, become one of the world's great powers in fine wine. It is interesting how often such changes are inspired by the determination and grit of one person. This is fully discussed in *The Conscience of Argentina* on page 147.

As wine producers looked for export markets, trade liberalization made money available from traditional sources. Above all, free trade meant re-thinking the whole approach to wine, and wine styles. Export markets did not want the type of wines enjoyed in Argentina. The market required global styles - and Argentina's own two charmers - Malbec and Torrontés.

Accordingly, the 1980s saw the start of a new chapter, not dissimilar to the mid-1800s. This time it was big money and state-of-the-art technology in many forms. All the technology was imported, as was much of the money. With a stable, if not very honest government, Argentina became once more a good place to invest. New money in the form of winery investment or take-overs came from Austria, Chile, France, Germany, Spain and the USA. Meanwhile technicians from  these countries, plus Australia and Italy, have been engaged at many wineries, especially in Mendoza province.

Today Argentina has two dominant wine types - domestic and international. The styles of the international wines are, indeed, international. As in any other wine exporting country, the Argentine export wines range from cheap to expensive. Generally, low priced super-market wines come from areas where land costs are cheap and production levels are high. In the case of domestic wines, production levels range from 30-50 tonnes (or more) per hectare, while export wines are in the range of 8 - 15 tonnes/ha.

Much of the domestic consumption is blended wine sold in *damjuana* or demi-johns. Bottled wine normally has a generic European name such as Borgoña.

Conversely, with the exception of vast quantities of bulk wine sold to winemakers in other countries, almost all export wine is varietal e.g. Cabernet, Malbec, Merlot, Chardonnay, Chenin, or Torrontés. These varietal styles differ enormously from heavily oaked to wines without oak.

A man and a woman, each with their own needs, taking delivery at Bodegas Norton.

41

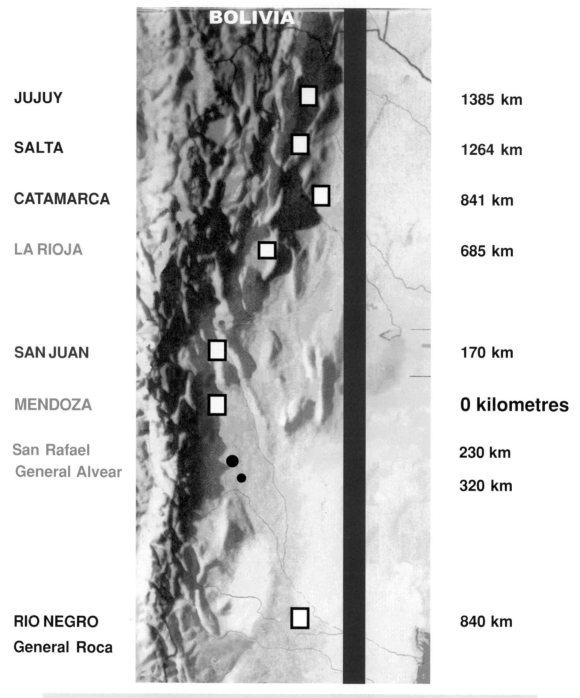

JUJUY   1385 km

SALTA   1264 km

CATAMARCA   841 km

LA RIOJA   685 km

SAN JUAN   170 km

MENDOZA   **0 kilometres**

San Rafael   230 km
General Alvear   320 km

RIO NEGRO   840 km
General Roca

Argentina has 1485 wineries registered with the official governent organization *Instituto Nacional de Vitivinicultura* (INV). From an international trading standpoint, there are less than 50.

Distribution of wineries by provinces is: Buenos Aires 7; Catamarca 17; Cordoba 7; La Rioja 38; Mendoza 1,063; Nequen 2; Rio Negro 41; Salta 15; San Juan 294; San Luis 1.

42

ARGENTINE WINE REGIONS

When referring to the wine regions of Argentina, one must, because of its giant size, draw a parallel with both California and Australia. In view of its location in the Southern Hemisphere and considerable similarities in desert-like growing conditions, Argentina would be wise to take Australia as a model. The Southern Hemisphere, unlike the Northern, is mainly oceans and deserts. In addition, there are no grapes indigenous to the countries in the south; all vines have been brought from the north. This has meant a dedicated research effort, an area in which Australia leads the world; research that Argentina desperately needs and cannot afford at this time.

Argentina is conveniently divided into three large regions, as diverse as any on earth:

1. The Andean north west, is unlike very much else on this planet;

2. The Cuyo has similarities to many fine wine regions;

3. The Southern region, in northern Patagonia, is a star waiting for its time.

The Andean North West is something else, the conditions and varieties are unique. Taking-in the provinces of Jujuy, Salta, Catamarca and La Rioja, which have boundaries with Chile, Bolivia and Paraguay, the vast region has the Tropic of Capricorn as its central point. This is definitely not the normal place to grow grapes for fine wine making. The elevation and proximity to the world's greatest mountain range is what makes fine wine possible. The vineyard with the lowest elevation in the region would exceed the highest vineyard in Australia. Just imagine the climate at 1,900 metres, nearly three times the height of Australia's highest!

Currently the Cuyo is Argentina's brightest star; all the money and muscle is there. Stretching from San Juan province to the Colorado River, this firmly established area has the benefit of several fine oenology schools and an INTA research station which has its own dedicated viti-vinicultural researchers.

There are many splendid areas and positive people doing good things in the Cuyo but one has the feeling that the vision of Argentina's potential is limited. Although new and better areas are being established within the Cuyo for fine wines, no-one is looking to the south for another source of complex grapes.

The south, as mentioned elsewhere, is a foreign country within a country but the potential to produce grapes of the highest quality is as certain as any place on earth. Great wines are made from superb weather conditions; not an annual occurrence. At most, they may happen only four or five times each decade. Most find this hard to comprend.

43

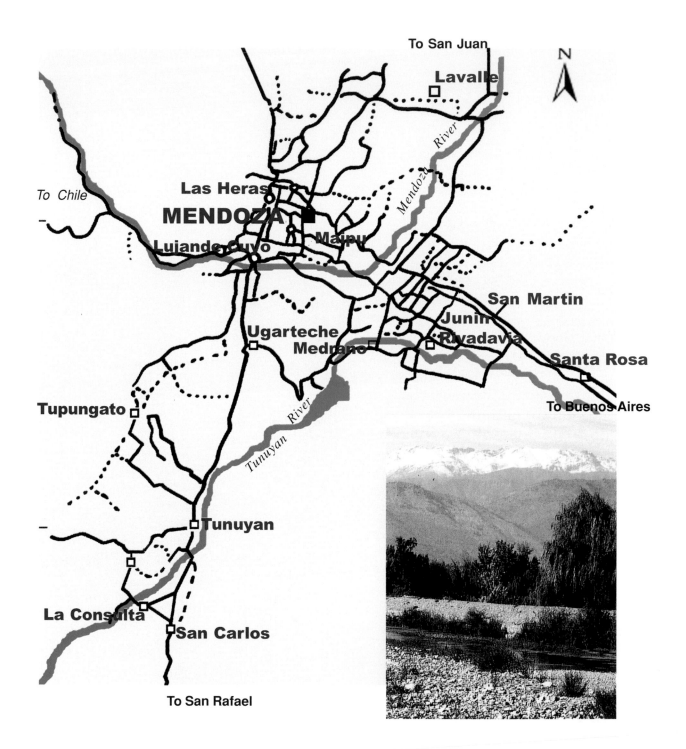

To San Juan

Lavalle

N

To Chile

Las Heras

MENDOZA

Lujan de Cuyo

Maipu

Mendoza River

San Martin

Junin
Rivadavia

Ugarteche
Medrano

Santa Rosa

To Buenos Aires

Tupungato

Tunuyan River

Tunuyan

La Consulta

San Carlos

To San Rafael

WINE REGIONS AROUND MENDOZA

44

MENDOZA

Situated at latitude 32.48° South, Mendoza is midway between the latitudes of CapeTown, South Africa, and Perth, Western Australia. In any language this spells hot summers and cold winters; perfect grapegrowing conditions.

As is the Spanish custom, the largest city, or the provincial Capital, is named for the province. To understand the local wine scene, Argentina has 23 *provinces* which are broken down into *departments;* these, again, are named after the largest *ciudad* (city) and they are further broken down into *districts*. A Mendoza province example is the *department* of Luján de Cuyo, with a city of the same name. The districts of Lujan department are Drummond, Las Compuertas, Blanco Encalada, Perdriel, La Colonia, Lunlunta, Carrodilla, Agrelo, Vistalba and Chacras de Coria.

Other departments within Mendoza province, all wine producers, are: Las Heras, Guaymallén, Valle (Valley) de Uco, Junín, San Martín, Lavalle and San Rafael.

A strange quirk of geography places Mendoza 1,040 km from the Federal Capital, Buenos Aires, but only 360 km from the Chilean capital, Santiago. Such is the power of natural barriers like mountains and rivers.

By whichever route the visitor reaches Mendoza, the traveler will find this city truly, an oasis. From the east, one can reach Mendoza by road, coach or air. Traveling from the west, the journey can be made by air or road. Neither of the railways over the Andes or from Buenos Aires, is still operating. Following the River Mendoza from the air is a sight one never forgets and a route strongly recommended; it provides a picture of the river's origins and destination. The road across the Andes from Mendoza, over the Uspallata Pass, to Santiago also follows the river's full distance. Only by following it can one gauge the Mendoza River's majesty and importance.

Argentines are a fun-loving people, and nowhere is this better exemplified than in the thriving oasis of Mendoza. Mendocinos, as they are known, enjoy a quality of life that is the envy of most visitors. However, this writer is fearful that Mendoza's fragile natural beauty is being polluted by exhaust emissions from motor vehicles of all types. Industrial discharges are fast becoming an urgent problem. It is not a very pretty sight when a pall of smog floats down the valley against the snow white backdrop of the Andes playground.

And what a playground the Andes is for Mendocinos and visitors! Besides the obvious skiing and mountain climbing/ trekking, there are many other adventure hobbies such as white water rafting, mountain biking, mule treks and an endless list of physical activities. For

45

the more sedate, there are beautiful parks, one of the world's largest wine festivals, a Tour de France look-alike cycle race, and a casino. University de Cuyo is an excellent tertiary institution.

Mendoza is a flourishing, lively city - and province. The city itself has 125,000 folks while *Gran* (Grand) *Mendoza* which includes Las Heras, Godoy Cruz and Guaymallen, totals 780,000, making it the nation's fourth largest city after Buenos Aires, Cordoba and Rosario. The provincial figure is given as 1.45 million.

The extensive irrigation system, developed and utilized by the Huarpe Indians probably 700 years ago, gravitates water from the majestic mountains and has benevolently provided this desert city with big trees including many sycamores. Attractive trees dominate the many parks, plazas, malls and streets of the city. Italian poplars can be seen along all the country lanes and water channels. It is nature's way of camouflaging an oasis! These elegant poplars, and their hybrids, provide much welcome shade for people and, importantly, for the vast network of irrigation channels. Trees also create needed shade and windbreaks for unsheltered vineyards.

Following the devastating 1861 earthquake which flattened the city, the area was re-peopled mainly by Italian emigrants. Today, Italian names dominate in the community while successive generations have adopted the bi-Spanish/Argentine culture and language. Obviously this background has dramatically changed the viticultural practices from Spanish to Italian, especially in the choice of grape varieties and vine-training methods.

Mendoza province is officialy credited with 1,063 wineries but the private sector says a more accurate figure of exporting wineries would be less than 50. These wineries vary enormously in production facilities, from the very latest technology to mainly concrete tank-type old-fashioned equipment. The greatest wines all over the world have, traditionally, been made in concrete tanks and large old oak casks - but their days are gone. A parallel would be that the horse and cart, still widely used in the Cuyo, is also an efficient mode of transport. Simply, tools of another time.

Everyone in Mendoza province (and Chile, also) has a grandstand view of the breath-taking Andes. From the Argentine side, it's a slow gradual ascent to the pass over the cordillera. The eastern Andean foot-hills and the valley floor spreading away to the east, provide an extensive range of carefully-chosen climatic conditions for viticulture; ranging from 600-1300 metres above sea level.

Although there is no government administered *appellation* system in place, there is a similar movement known as *denominación de origen* in three Mendoza regions: Maipu, Lujan de Cuyo and San Rafael. (There is another in La Rioja). What these people are trying to achieve is honesty in labeling, a statement saying that the wine in the bottle is from this or that particular region. Certainly, this is being done in good faith. Nevertheless it is at a time when the wine buyer the world over knows that these schemes may simply be marketing gimmicks and mean little or, even worse, nothing. Honesty in labeling is in the hearts of men, not in an obscure, well-intentioned committee.

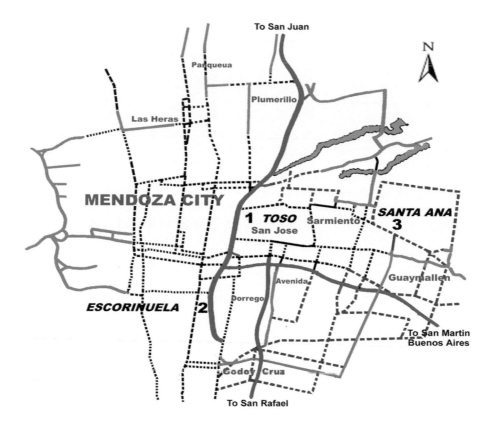

To San Juan

Panqueua

Plumerillo

N

Las Heras

MENDOZA CITY

1 TOSO
San Jose

Sarmiento

SANTA ANA
3

Avenida

Guaymallen

ESCORIHUELA 2

Dorrego

To San Martin
Buenos Aires

Godoy Crua

To San Rafael

GRAN MENDOZA

Visitors to Escorihuela winery enjoyng the regular art and sculpture exhibition.

On the facing page, Escorihuela of the 1920s. Above, Escorihuela today - on the outside only the vehicles have changed - everything has changed inside the many walls.

Author's Choice

Cabernet Sauvignon

Vineyards:

Los Castaños, Tupungato: Chardonnay, Riesling Renano, Gewurztraminer, Pinot blanc. Merlot

Los Nietos, Tupungato: Riesling Renano Cabernet Sauvignon & Franc,Merlot, Malbec

Los Sobrinos, Rivadavia: 43 ha Chenin

La Fundadora, Maipu: 9 ha Cabernet Sauvignon

Domestic labels:

San Felipe, Pequeña Vasija, R.F.N., Felipe Rutini

ESCORIHUELA
(Ess-cor-ee-whale-ah)

Located at 1180 Belgrano in Godoy Cruz, just two blocks from the main thoroughfare Avenida San Martin, Escorihuela is only 3-4 minutes by car from downtown Mendoza, making it one of the most central bodegas for the wine tourist. This is really upper suburban Mendoza and it is difficult to imagine that, at one time, the area was covered with vineyards.

Besides the highest quality wines, Escorihuela offers a marvelous self-guided classy art exhibition which changes monthly throughout the year. The gallery entrance is actually the reception area of the old home with floors of black and white marble fronting  onto a courtyard on one side. The former drawing and dining rooms are on the other side where the paintings are hung. Sculpture is displayed in the gallery-reception section.

The sight of large groups of school children who regularly visit the winery would send a chill down the back of many Americans. While religion intrudes into almost every phase of Argentine life, the mania about alcohol is an American phenomenon; we all have our strange ways.

Besides the Escorihuela label, there are Pinar del Rio, a non-vintage white blend, and a 100 percent Cabernet Carcassone which has a sister white blend of Chenin and Chardonnay. Now the top-of-the-range Pont l'Eveque label will feature 100% Viognier white and a 100% Malbec, arguably Argentina's best. The Viognier wine is a top indicator wine.

Founded in 1884 by Miguel Escorihuela Gascón, it was passed onto his Spanish nephews in 1920. When acquired by Nicolas Catena in early 1992 a completely new equipment modernization program was immediately instituted. Escorihuela is one of Mendoza's oldest wineries, the buildings are enormous and occupy several blocks of valuable real estate. Consistent with Mendoza's growth and sophistication, fortunately a top class international restaurant is now under construction.

Many of the Catena group wines can be purchased at the on-site retail store, including wines made by overseas contractors. Tours available Monday-Friday at 9.00, 10.30, 11.30, 12.30, 13.00 and 15.30 daily.

49

LOPEZ

Despite rebuilding a very modern bodega to celebrate their centenary, Lopez could be classified as one of the rocks on which Mendoza was built. And, despite two young brothers at the helms of administration and winemaking, Lopez will continue as a traditional Mendoza bodega. Eduardo Lopez Laurenz is the administrative director and his brother, Carlos Alberto, heads up the winemaking side of the business.

There is no way they are going to be herded into these fancy varietal wines or labels, if it ain't broke why fix it could be the Lopez slogan for the future. In a rather strange twist for a family of Andelusian-Spanish descent, they have several wines with French chateau names e.g. Chateau Vieux, Chateau Monchenot and Mont Reims.

Like so many others, José López Rivas was driven out of Europe in the mid-19th century by the disease phylloxera, a little bug that devastated European vineyards. (Phylloxera is still rampant in Argentina but is held in check by the flood irrigation — phylloxera does not like water). He arrived in Argentina with only living expenses and commenced work selling grapes into Buenos Aires. Having earned the money to bring his family to their new-found home, the family moved to Mendoza and became established in vinicululture. Then the move to selling bulk wine in barrels — as was the case the world over until World War 11.

From their new farm in General Gutiérrez, Maipu, the Lopez family established *Marilen* olive oil and Selección Lopez wine products that are still the backbone of the company today and are distributed to supermarkets, restaurants, wholesalers and distributors throughout Argentina. Their international markets for wine and olive oil are spread throughout Latin America, the USA, Germany and Austria.

Visits by appointment only.

50

PASCUAL TOSO

While not still financially controlled by the family, third and fourth generations of the Toso family are still managing the company's Mendoza operations. Established four generations ago in 1890, the San Jose bodega is but six blocks from the centre of downtown Mendoza. One of the four streets around the winery is named for the founder, Pascual Toso. Until 1940, Toso had vineyards right in town when urban pressures forced them to move the winery to their 300 ha vineyard in Barrancas, 42 km from the city, which had been purchased in 1907.

There are 160 ha planted at Barrancas with Cabernet, Malbec, Merlot, Syrah, while Chardonnay, Sauvignon and Torrontes Riojana make up the whites. These vines are being upgraded with American rootstocks and new scions from Italy and France. Required grapes are purchased from local Barrancas growers because Toso believe this is where the majority of old vines are located.

Currently vineyard work and most winemaking is done in Barrancas, all bottling and the sparkling wines are made at the San Jose site. Toso has a collection of standard varietal wines for both export and domestic markets. With 30 years experience, Toso is one of Argentina's oldest exporters which they say was once a very unprofitable business. Apparently all export payments had to be made to the government who serenely took their big share before passing the leftovers to the exporting winery! Their main markets nowadays are in the UK, followed by Scandinavia, Germany and Holland. Most popular export wines are Cabernet and Syrah, their experience is that while people talk about Malbec, they go away and buy Cabernet.

Toso sparkling wines are made from a Chardonnay/Chenin base wine. Wines fermented in tanks by the Charmat method are sold as sparkling wines with enough residual sugar to please local winelovers. Sparklers made using the traditional method are sold as Champagne. Toso wines are well-made and extremely good value.

CHARDONNAY

TOSO

VINO FINO BLANCO

ELABORADO
Y ENVASADO
EN ORIGEN POR
S.A. INDUSTRIAL
Y AGRICOLA
PASCUAL TOSO

ALBERDI 808
SAN JOSE
GUAYMALLEN
MENDOZA - INSC.
I.N.V. N° A - 74270
D.I. 111

CONT. NETO

INDUSTRIA ARGENTINA 700cm3 PROCEDENCIA MENDOZA

ENVASADO EN ORIGEN

51

Author's Choice

Malbec

José Alberto Zuccardi

A dazzling array of labels from a winery as modern as tomorrow.

LA AGRICOLA

(lah - ag - RICKola)

La Agricola is one of Argentina's most progressive wine producers and aggressive wine marketers who have developed a strong international profile. They can be seen at trade shows around the globe right alongside the "big boys". This is reflected in the fact that they are one of the few Argentine companies who sell more by export than on the home market.

This is a company with wonderful people, an attitude set by example from the top. Alberto Zuccardi's parents arrived in Argentina two generations before he decided, in 1963, to start in the grape growing business. Alberto was joined in 1976 by his son José Alberto who now runs this thriving wine company, allowing Alberto to enjoy semi-retirement - while retaining an interest in all around him.

With over 430 ha of productive vineyards, this is not a small operation, but will only become larger when growth can be properly managed. The home vineyards of 170ha surrounding the 14 million litre winery are a showpiece, highlighted by spectacular anti-hail nets. Another 240ha of vineyards are away to the east at Santa Rosa. Being located on the vast plains, it is to hoped that one day soon, La Agricola will bring white wine grapes from vineyards higher into the Andes.

José Alberto and his neighbours have banded together to overcome the major problem of hail by the use of Russian anti-hail rockets. When hail threatens, the rockets are launched to a height of eight - 12 kilometres thus dispersing the hail into almost harmless, rain-like drops.

La Agricola has a wide, colorful and artistic set of labels for their many brands which mirror the tireless and ebullient export director, Cecilia Fernandez, one of the remarkable people in the world of wine.

As a sign of their ongoing commitment to quality, La Agricola has engaged the services of not one, but two New World consultants.

La Agricola's wide range of interesting wines is aimed at the everyday consumer, people who like to enjoy wine with their daily food. I'll drink to that! In José Alberto's own words, "We offer good value-for-money relationship".

This is unquestioned and the Company's innovative nature sees them with such interesting labels as Bonarda, Tempranilla and Torrontes, all varieties that can be mass produced at very reasonable prices. Then there is the top range of Malbec, Cabernet, Chardonnay, Sauvignon and other interesting wines - no-one could ask for more.

53

Pedro Marchevski

Vineyards:

Agrelo: Chardonnay, Sauvignon, Semillon, Viognier

Cabernet S., Malbec, Merlot, Sangiovese, Syrah, Barbera, Pinot Noir

Ugarteche: Chardonnay, Cabernet S., Pinot N.

Lunlunta: Chardonnay, Cabernet S., Malbec.

Tupungato: Currently being planted with Chardonnay, Pinot noir, Merlot

La Consulta: Chardonnay, Riesling, Merlot.

Domestic labels: Generic wines - Valderrobles Borgoño, Beaujolais and Chablis,

Varietals - Valderrobles Cabernet, Riesling.

Saint Felicien - Cabernet Sauvignon, Cabernet/ Merlot,

Saint Felician - Chardonnay with and without oak maturation.

Shorthorn Malbec, Shorthorn Saugvignon (blanc).

Export labels:

Catena - Cabernet Sauvignon, Chardonnay, Malbec.

Catena Alto - Cabernet Sauvignon and Chardonnay.

Alamos Ridge - Cabernet and Chardonnay

Author's Choice

Catena Alta Chardonnay

Paul Hobbs and Jorge Catena

54

ESMERALDA

Although each star shines brightly, Esmeralda (emerald) could rightly be classified as the brightest star in Catena-Zapata group's varied constellation. Being situated in Junin department, it is one of the more difficult for the traveler to locate, therefore Esmeralda is not geared to the tourist trade. Fortunately, Esmeralda's domestic counterpart wines, under the Valderrobles and Saint Felicien labels, are available at good wine stores throughout Argentina. The Catena label and another less expensive range, Alamos Ridge, are wines for export only. From a strong base Catena exports grew an amazing 50 percent annually during the mid 90s.

Unfortunately, the philosophy of many Argentine winemakers is to drive forward while looking through the rear vision mirror. In winemaking terms this means that old is good, and very old must be extremely good. This mentality is symbolized in much wine literature, almost everything is named after generations past and the images are of an era long departed. No doubt this fits well into an Italian-Spanish culture, but is heavy baggage in today's New World wine markets.

Following Nicolas Catena's return home from a 1976 California visit, younger brother Jorge enrolled for enology courses at University of California, Davis (UCD). His homecoming awakened a new generation for the Catena winery and signalled to all Argentina wineries what the possibilities were in this blessed land. New technology was introduced into the winery - and the varietals Cabernet and Chardonnay became the Holy Grail. The company regards this period as the turning point in its history.

At UCD, Jorge met fellow student, Paul Hobbs. In 1988, Hobbs accepted the role of visiting consultant for fine wine production, specifically Cabernet and Chardonnay, at Esmeralda winery. With Hobbs' arrival to assist Jorge Catena and the very talented enologist, José Galante, the old mentality quickly departed from Esmeralda, as did two Italian winemaking signatures, big, old oak casks and concrete tanks. Today the winery is as efficient and modern as any in the New World. The barrel room is quite a sight for even the most critical observer.

Only five years would pass before their wine had international acceptance. Catena Chardonnay was chosen as 1993 World Champion Moderately-Priced White Wine (price US$12.39). With 97 points out of a possible 100, the Chardonnay had the same rating as the World's Premium-Priced White Wine (US$28.00).

When one considers that this category included all white wines such as Char-

55

donnay, Sauvignon, Semillon, Pinot gris, Viognier and blends, and these coming from around the world, this was a notable success. The high score of 97 points rated a Platinum Medal. Seventy other wines were awarded the lesser gold medal.

This was not a one time success. On another occasion at the New York Wine Experience, an event involuntarily attended by the who's who of global wine, the Catena Chardonnay was a featured wine. In a blind evaluation of international wines, the majority of the cognoscenti agreed that the Catena wine was an expensive white Burgundy from France. Many wine critics, including this writer, think along similar lines.

These achievements have only encouraged Nicolas Catena to push the quality limits towards infinity with all varieties of interest - and this certainly includes a stunning Malbec, arguably one of Argentina's finest wines.

The work of a consultant is to come and go as needed, yet for 12 months of the year somebody must hold the reigns in the vineyard and winery. Esmeralda is indeed fortunate in having Pedro Marchevski as production chief. As passionate about wine as his boss, Pedro is fanatical regarding grape quality and the overall role of the vineyard in wine quality. It is his position to supervise the year-round calendar of experiments being conducted in the winery, and, probably the most complex set of vineyards in Argentina. Pedro has incredible support in this pursuit of excellence

Esmeralda could be classified as a large scale test tube operation. While some have great expectations, nobody knows

what potential Argentina's wine growing regions and winemakers can ultimately reach. Nicolas Catena desires to make his contribution in many practical ways.

Situated in Mendoza's prime locations, the Catena group vineyards are rapidly approaching a time when the winery will be able to offer a wide selection of relatively new varieties more suited to local conditions, rather than the Cabernet/Chardonnay stampede.

The money, work, thought and effort that go into these vineyards are of a level that most can only dream about. Nobody in the world monitors each vineyard with such intense scrutiny as the Catena people; they believe in reality, not lip service as is so very common. This professionalism is obvious in the finished wines.

Only grapes from the company's own vineyards are used in the wines. Varieties such as Sangiovese, Syrah, Semillon and Viognier from these vineyards will be among Argentina's frontline wines of the 21st century. These exciting varieties, along with Barbera, are well worth the extended wait, but this time is rapidly approaching.

Catena/Esmeralda wines can only be classified as world class and incredible value - and the Alamos Ridge range features good value-for-money wines.

As this book goes to press, the winery is about to release, in limited quantities, something very special. The Catena Alta super premium range of Malbec, Cabernet Sauvignon and Chardonnay. will have winelovers the world over seeing Argentina's real potential.

56

MENDOZA WINE ZONES

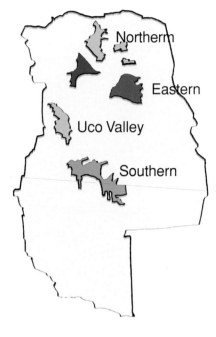

MENDOZA PROVINCE

A decade ago, those wonderful people at INTA Central Enology Study centre devised a method of classifying the wine regions of Mendoza province based on location and elevation. They determined five regions, three of which are close-in to the capital. The *northern* and *eastern* zones are respectively north and east of the city and furthest from the Andes, being below 650 metres are lowest in elevation.

The high zone of the Mendoza River embraces the departments of Lujan de Cuyo, Maipu, Guaymallen and Las Heras; only the departments of Lujan and Maipu are relative to this text.

The two other zones determined were the *Uco Valley* zone and *southern* zone, the areas around San Rafael. Each zone has also, loosely, been given a number by somebody; the high zone is also known as the primary, or #1 zone.

For the sake of geographical ease and to avoid any more confusion, each department will be dealt with individually.

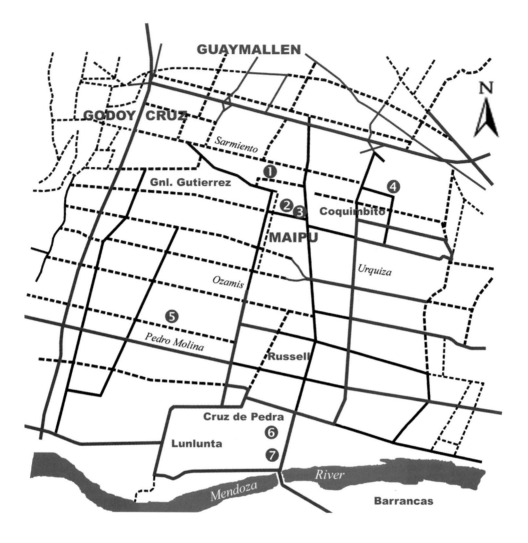

WINERIES OF MAIPU

Position: 32.48S 68.45W

	Bodega	Address	Town
1	Fecovito	Carril Gomez 265	Gnl. Gutierruz
2	Lopez	Ozamis 375	Gnl. Gutierrez
3	Trapiche	Nueva Mayorga s/n	Coquimbito
4	La Rural	Montecaseros s/n	Coquimbito
5	Navarro Correas	Juan B Custo s/n	Gnl Gutierrez
6	Martins Domingos	Calle Nueva s/n	Cruz de Piedra
7	San Telmo	Pescara s/n	Cruz de Pedra

MAIPU DEPARMENT

Contains: City of Maipu; Grl Gutiérrez; Coquimbito; Fray Luis Beltran; Russel, Lunlunta, Cruz de Piedra, Barrancas.

Prior to the railway line and earthquake there was little in the way of vineyards outside the Mendoza settlement. These two major events caused a flood of re-settlement and vineyards started to crop-up out-of-town, initially in the direction of Maipu.

The department of Maipu is a mass of contradictions. It was a long haul from 1858 when the department was founded until it became a city of sorts in 1942. One of Mendoza's smallest departments in size, it contains two of the world's largest wineries. The 135,000 population don't seem to get excited about very much besides the three national religions: soccer football, cigarettes and Roman Catholicism. As in many other departments, olives were an integral a part of the family farm whether they be Spanish or Italian settlers; often equal numbers of olive and vine rows. Consequently, Maipu still has a strong olive oil industry, a product very dear to the hearts and tummies of Mendocinos.

At a mean average of 800 metres above sea level and an average rainfall of 190mm, Maipu department is a strong and good red wine region. Among the 1,688 vineyards, red varieties total almost 5,000 ha and whites about 4,000. The prime variety in the region is rightfully Malbec which represents 37 percent of all red plantings. Cabernet at 700 ha is not very far ahead of the ordinary Bonarda at 680 ha with the 580 ha of Tempranilla, mistakenly considered as an insignificant variety, not far behind. Sangiovese, an also-ran in terms of quality, has 450 ha.

Maipu has a lot of re-thinking to do as to the value of the varieties available - and should stop pouring water onto varieties that could be a quality, rather than quantity, and become personal signatures of the region. These are the right varieties in the right region with a potential to make extremely good wines in Maipu, yet only one varietal Sangiovese and no Tempranillo wines comes out of the district. These excellent Italian and Spanish varieties are being executed on the cross of mediocrity, being blended away to the lowest common denominator; a sad indictment. With nearly 4,200 ha, the largest planted category are the varieties criollas and cerezas muscatel which are used for local consumption Rose wine. Total red plantings cover 4,700 ha.

In Maipu department white grapes occupy over 3,800 ha representing 30 percent of plantings. There are nearly 500 ha of the desirable Chenin and mor then 350 ha of Chardonnay. Unfortunately for the future, the overhead parral sytem of vine training represents more than 60 percent all grapes planted in Maipu.One day soon these grapes will have to be mechanically harvested.

59

Vineyards:

Los Castaños, Tupungato: Chardonnay, Riesling Renano, Gewurztraminer, Pinot blanc.   Merlot

Los Nietos, Tupungato: Riesling Renano Cabernet Sauvignon & Franc, Merlot, Malbec

Los Sobrinos, Rivadavia: 43 ha Chenin

La Fundadora, Maipu: 9 ha Cabernet Sauvignon

Domestic labels:

San Felipe, Pequeña Vasija, R.F.N., Felipe Rutini

Rodolfo Reina Rutini, President, La Rural, and author of a book on Mendoza's wine history.

Author's Choice

Rutini Cabernet Sauvignon

Cowskin used in earlier days for wine production

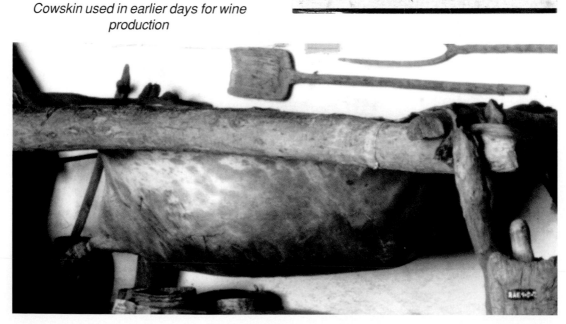

LA RURAL

Although established in 1885, today La Rural is one of Argentina's most sophisticated wineries. Don't be fooled by the old carts and antiquities on the winery grounds, or the superb wine museum. Inside the winery La Rural is as modern as tomorrow.

Felipe Rutini graduated from agricultural college in Italy in 1883 and only two years later founded La Rural in the Maipu village of Coquimbito. La Rural is still presided over by one of his great grandsons. As part of the Catena-Zapata group La Rural enjoys technical input from a wide range of consultants from around the world and this surely shows in the wine.

Of particular interest is the fact that the Rutini family "discovered" the now famous Tupungato region two generations ago. Here they planted Chardonnay and Merlot long before the world heard of them as varietal wines. These were blended away into the flagship generic wine, San Felipe, which features packaging in the traditional Franconian Rose bottle.

Today, the San Felipe white wine is a blend of Chardonnay and Chenin while the red wine is a blend of Malbec and Merlot. This and other domestic labels are popular in South America, Paraguay in particular. Winelovers in North America will find both Trumpeter and top-of-the-line Rutini labels on the shelves at their local supermarkets and fine wine stores. The Rutini label currently has an excellent Chardonnay and, arguably, Argentina's best Malbec. The Trumpeter wines include Cabernet, Malbec, Merlot and Chardonnay.

EEC wine aficionados have a choice of the Rutini, La Rural and Libertad labels. The La Rural wines are Malbec and Merlot varietals and the white is an interesting blend of two diverse varietals, Chardonnay and Pinot blanc; certainly a first in South America. Export wines are in claret and burgundy bottles.

Visitors are welcome at La Rural and the guided tour includes one of the best winery museums in the country, a wine and accessories store, plus tastings on six weekdays (holiday Sundays) 0900-1200 and 1500-1900.

61

TRAPICHE®
Malbec
OAK CASK

"Estate bottled in Mendoza.
Remarkable for its lively colour,
sweet aroma of black fruit confiture
and dry taste with volume and structure.
This Malbec was aged in new French oak
bringing an elegant touch of smoke
and vanilla candy. Ready to drink,
its best years lie ahead."

Produced & bottled by Bodegas Trapiche
Mendoza . Argentina

13 % alc. by vol.   750 ML

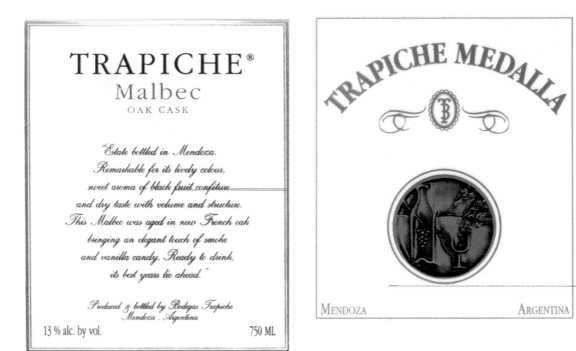

TRAPICHE MEDALLA

MENDOZA   ARGENTINA

Author's Choice

A good range of well-made wines -
Oak Cask Malbec is easy drinking!

MENDOZA   ARGENTINA

Since 1883

Fond de Cave
CHARDONNAY

WHITE WINE PRODUCED & BOTTLED BY
BODEGAS TRAPICHE MENDOZA ARGENTINA

13% alc. by vol.   750 ML

TRAPICHE®

Since 1883

Estate Bottled
Mendoza

Cabernet Sauvignon

Produced & bottled by Bodegas Trapiche
Mendoza · Argentina

13% alc by vol.   750 ML

April Rose
Rosé of Cabernet Sauvignon

Since 1885

TRAPICHE

Produced & bottled by Bodegas Trapiche
Mendoza · Argentina

12% alc by vol.   750 ML

TRAPICHE

Following California's Gallo winery and the KWV Cooperative of South Africa, Peñaflor is reputedly the world's third largest winery - and owns the world's largest wine blending tank, five million litres or more! That is the ogre Trapiche is trying to remove from its back, the ogre of giant size. Supposedly they are two different companies, but, until recently, had the same ownership and the same address.

As the Pulenta family are loathe to make themselves available for interview, nor answer any pertinent correspondence, one must rely on other reliable sources. However, they have admitted to a purge within the family and Trapiche is now owned by a group headed by Luis A. Pulenta

With their refinery-sized wineries in San Juan and Maipu, the family have traditionally been makers of vast amounts of the popular, everyday drinking wines. After purchasing Trapiche in 1970 from the famous Benegas family, the Pulentas decided on a course that would make them Argentina's largest exporters. In those days they did this well with aggressive marketing and reasonably good wines at fair prices.

Like Gallo and KWV, the Pulentas have been astute enough to realize that they could do much better in the upmarket quality wine arena. To this end they hired outstanding Australian viticulturist, Richard Smart, to put their vineyards and viticultural thinking in order; a smart move. For some strange reason, they also brought a consultant winemaker from the lush, unirrigated vineyards of Bordeaux, France, to make wine in a southern hemisphere desert; bizarre!

This French connection is reflected in their wine, Medalla, which exceeds 80 percent Cabernet Sauvignon in a region renowned for its own distinctive Malbec - a grape that makes up only eight percent of this blend; even more bizarre! Cabernet, when you can have Malbec?

In October 1997, a prestigious UK wine magazine made an interesting comment, *"Many observers find it difficult to understand why Trapiche does not make Argentina's best wine."* It is fair to suggest that this giant can do as it pleases, but one would think that it has a responsibility to Argentina, and the wine industry, to be a leader, rather than a follower.

Dr. Smart has ensured that the 1,800 ha of vineyards have the right grape varieties planted in the right regions and this allows the company to have the very best raw materials.

Trapiche can, and will be, to Argentina what Penfold's is to Australia - one of the few great, large wine companies of the world. They have all the basic resources - but great wine is an obsession of dedicated people - not the bottom line on a balance sheet dictated by accountants or family greed. When great wine is made, winelovers are prepared to pay the price.

63

Finca (farm) Flichman, Barrancas, above. Classic stoney soils of the Mendoza River, below.

Author's Choice

Syrah is a favorite among some very good reds.

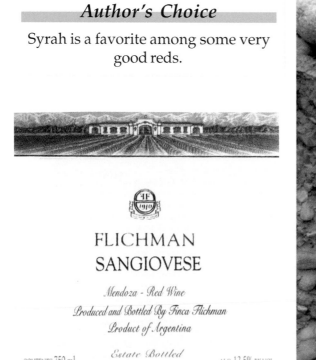

FLICHMAN
SANGIOVESE

Mendoza - Red Wine

Produced and Bottled By Finca Flichman
Product of Argentina

Estate Bottled

CONTENTS 750 ml.   ALC 12,5% BY VOL.

FLICHMAN

Sami Flichman was a downtown Mendoza clothes merchant who in 1910 became part of the rural life by purchasing a defunct winery in the Maipu region of Barrancas. The first thing that strikes a visitor to the modern day Flichman winery is the gracious setting amongst an olive grove and giant, shady eucalyptus trees. The estate house and the winery have also been carefully maintained in their turn-of-the-20th century estancia type architecture by the new owners.

The Werthein family, wealthy cattle ranchers from the Pampas who have extended their business to banking, insurance, food and farming, purchased Finca Flichman in 1983. They virtually gutted the winery and replaced old-fashioned equipment with state of the art machinery and technology — within the confines of the naturally insulated adobe mud walls. Much of the old machinery and tools have been carefully preserved and form part of an interesting museum.

Finca Flichman is a fascinating estate in that it is one of very few that has all its 200 ha of vineyards surrounding the winery. The farm has another 400 ha to develop and this will be done in annual increments of 50 hectares. This has been made possible by the use of drip irrigation instead of the wasteful flood-style watering which is common on the flat lands of Maipu. Vines can only be planted to the amount of water available to the farm - no water, no vines. Recognizing the eventual need for vineyard mechanization, all new plantings are on American rootstocks and will be trained to the vertical shoot positioning trellis, a system that is fast replacing the traditional overhead parral-type trellising.

The Barrancas soil is strikingly similar to Chateauneuf du Pape in France's southern Rhone region and it is obvious that like varieties should be planted in this region. Flichman have taken heed of this message with plantings of Syrah and Sangiovese which are ideally suited to the terroir. Other varieties include Cabernet, Malbec, Merlot and several whites unsuited to the climate or soils.

Flichman purchase grapes from selected growers in Lujan and Maipu to enable them to meet the needs of their one milllion case production, 20 percent of which goes to the export market. The company's strongest export markets are in the U.K., Scandinavia, USA, Japan and Holland. Their top export product is the Caballero de La Cepa Cabernet Sauvignon — a mighty fine bottle of wine originally developed by the Flichman family. Very engaging work is being done with the variety Syrah which, in time, could become Argentina's second red wine.

65

Author's Choice

Chardonnay

One more stunning view of the Andes from the Navarro Correas vineyard.

NAVARRO CORREAS

With major changes of ownership in 1997, the Argentine wine industry went through a watershed year. Navarro Correas was very much to the fore being taken over by the giant International Distillers and Vintners (IDV) group.

Having managed the Navarro Correas label for some years previous to the takeover, IDV had already made this one of the three most professional marketing wineries in the country.

Juan Correas planted vines in 1798, became governor of Mendoza in 1824 and was a bosom pal of the great General San Martin. That is about as far as anyone could go in the province. Successive generations of his family carried on the wine tradition. However, Navarro Correas as a wine label, did not arrive on the shelves until 1978.

As could be expected, the company has good vineyards in some of the best regions, Russel, Barrancas and a relatively small (15 ha) vineyard at Los Arboles in Tupungato region. While the plantings of Pinot noir in the warm Maipu areas of Russell and Barancas may puzzle many non-Argentine observers, the company is very strong in the sparkling wine business for which Pinot noir is a sound base wine. However, they do have a Pinot red wine from these vineyards and that does raise some questions of style.

Navarro Correas has an eye-boggling range of well-packaged, attractively labelled wines which are very specialized. From their red wine bodega in Rusell, under the Navarro Correas label, winemaker Alfredo Despous produces a Cabernet Sauvignon (Private Collection), Pinot noir, Syrah and Malbec. Under the Correas label comes an interesting blend of Syrah-Sangiovese and varietal Malbec, Syrah and Cabernet.

Skilled white winemaker, Rubén Sfagara, produces a barrel-fermented Chardonnay and night-harvested Sauvignon Fume for the top label and a Torrontes-Chardonnay blend for the Correas bottling. The white bodega facility is located at General Gutiérrez.

The sparkling wine (champaña) facility in Godoy Cruz has been supervised by the Deutz company of Reims, France, for some years. In fact, one of the sparkling labels carries a *Champagne Deutz, Francia* tag. In the competent hands of winemaker Enrique Antolin, a lot of good bubbly, but certainly not French, is coming from Godoy Cruz.

With production exceeding 150,000 cases annually, and increasing, this is hardly a small operation as claimed.

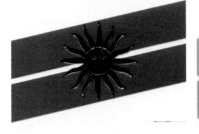

1997	1997	1997
CHARDONNAY	SAUVIGNON BLANC	MALBEC
WHITE WINE PRODUCT OF ARGENTINA	WHITE WINE PRODUCT OF ARGENTINA	RED WINE PRODUCT OF ARGENTINA

Author's Choice

Reds are the strong suit, Syrah and
Malbec in particular.

Martin's winemaker, Susana Balbo.

Martins

In a way, winemaking is very much like painting. Winemakers, like painters, start with a range of basic materials. In the case of winemakers they are soil, climate, vines, grapes and equipment within the bodega Yet, the essential basic elements of soil and climate can change within a kilometre, let alone across a giant mountain range, a desert or ocean. A Chardonnay grape grown in Lujan de Cuyo or just 100 km or so over the Andes in Chile will provide different flavors to the same variety grown in nearby San Juan or faraway Cafayate.

Inside the winery, to achieve the same end of a sound, flavorsome wine, the possibilities are endless. Fermentation tanks of concrete, stainless steel or oak casks, centrifuges, diatomaceous earth filters, tank presses, vertical drainers - the options are endless.

Everything is different about the Martins winemaking operation; the winery is certainly limited to very basic epoxy-coated concrete tanks and little else in the way of sophisticated winemakers toys. Nonetheless, what is really different about Martins are two women - one is the wine Evita, the other is Susana Balbo, winemaker-manager.

A dedicated professional, Susana works under the most rudimentary conditions to produce sound commercial wines from the popular varieties such as Malbec, Merlot, Cabernet, Chardonnay and Sauvignon. One wonders what would be possible with equipment that her colleagues have in nearby wineries. Being married to former university viticultural professor and Catena guru, Pedro Marchevsky, she has many opportunities to evaluate and discuss Argentina's best wines on a regular basis. This experience shows in Martin's wines which are good, sound, commercial wines.

As the winery produces more than 100,000 cases annually and is a strong player in the Argentina market, it surely is time for the winery to be refurbished in line with the quality of their magazine advertising. Despite these shortcomings, and the need to use oak planks joined together with food grade plastic clips, some of the reds are excellent. The Syrah and Malbec are worthy wines.

Only recently, distribution has been taken over by the major Spanish company Berberana and this now finds Martins wines in the U.K., Holland, German, Belgium and US markets.

The wine, Evita, is the brain-child of San Francisco importer, Ed Everett who has designed a sleek, black label. The wine is available nationally in the USA, Canada and Asia.

69

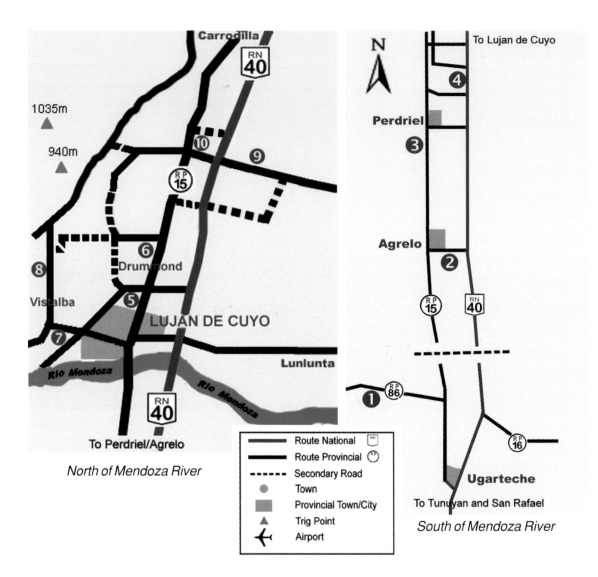

North of Mendoza River

South of Mendoza River

	Route National	RN
	Route Provincial	RP
----	Secondary Road	
●	Town	
▨	Provincial Town/City	
▲	Trig Point	
✈	Airport	

Wineries of Lujan de Cuyo

	Bodega	Address	District
1.	Viñas de Tupungato	RP 86	Ugarteche
2.	Chandon SA	Ruta Prov.15- Km 29	Agrelo
3.	Norton	Ruta Prov.15 - Km 23	Perdriel
4.	Arnaldo Etchart	Ruta 40 Km 22	Pedriel
5.	Leoncio Arizu	San Martin 2044	Drummond
6.	Lagarde SA	San Martin 1745	Drummond
7.	Dom. Vistalba	Saenz Peña s/n	Vistalba
8.	Casa Nieto y Senetiner	Vieja s/n	Vistalba
9.	Nieto y Senetiner	Vieytes s/n	Carrodilla
10.	Cavas de Weinert	San Martin 5923	Carrodilla

LUJAN DE CUYO

(Loo-han day Coo-joe)

Contains: City of Lujan, Agrelo, Carrizal, Carrodilla, Chacras de Coria, Drummond, Las Compuertas, La Puntilla, Perdriel, Potrerillas, Ugarteche, Vistalba

Lujan is one of several Argentine wine regions with abundant charm that makes one forget that this is the middle of a desert. While the department of Lujan de Cuyo straddles the Mendoza River, the city of 85,000 people which is situated on the north side, has the true stamp of sophistication.

Even though Lujan is only 20 kms from Mendoza city, it lacks nothing in the way of shopping or service facilities - and is free of Mendoza's traffic problems; for how long is another question. Mendoza is moving to Lujan in a big way, Chacras de Coria in particular.

Hopefully, this urban movement will bring to the area some new hotels and restaurants. At the moment the region is poorly served, except for the reasonable ACA restaurant at Cipoletto dam.

The tree-lined streets of the city are friendly places for visitors and residents. Even in the middle of screaming midsummer temperatures, Lujan seems to be cool. Further out into the country lanes of Lujan the big sycamores have been there long enough to arch across the roads and provide a large tunnel of beauty and welcome shade.

Within this affluent department there is an oil refinery and chemical plant puffing out pollution that the area doesn't need. This is balanced by the spectacular Cipollitto dam, a vast expanse of liquid gold from the Andes that provides for the area's water needs.

The region varies in altitude from 850 metres above sea level on the plains of Carrodilla to 1,350 metres at Potrerillas, which is on the international highway to Chile. This range of heights allows a diversity of crops, other than vines, to enrich the fare of Lujan. Notable among these other crops are apples and cherries which attest to a cool climate, peaches, tomatoes and garlic. The area also boasts cattle, pigs and chickens among its commercial livestock - a veritable cornucopia!

Vineyard locations vary from 900-1050 metres, making Lujan the epicentre of premium winegrowing in Mendoza province. This has attracted most of the major players to plant vineyards in the area - if not to build wineries. In the near future winelovers the world over will be as familiar with the vineyards of Agrelo, Carrodilla, Perdriel, Vistalba and Ugarteche as they are now with Coonawarra, Sonoma, Burgundy or the Rheinpfalz.

Author's Choice

Syrah

Alberto and Gustavo Arizu at trade show

LEONCIO ARIZU

For more than a century, the Arizu family have been large landholders and leaders in the Argentine viti-vinicultural business and show no signs of relinquishing this leadership. The pioneering Spanish family established vineyards in Maipu and Villa Atuel, near San Rafael, where they had the world's largest vineyard. At the beginning of the 20th century, a nephew, Leoncio, the one with whom we are concerned, established his holding in Lujan de Cuyo.

At the dawn of the 21st century and four generations later, the family have 400 ha of vineyards in Lujan and nearby Maipu, a dynamic organization, a clear view of the future and fine wines.

Obviously the founder knew good vineyard land when choosing Vistalba for his first buy. Wisely he bought further into Lujan, acquiring properties in La Puntilla, Carrodilla and the Finca Don Saturnino also in Lujan. El Paraíso is a specialized red wine vineyard in Maipu. The matching of grape varieties with the particular vineyard sites has always been a top priority, so it is strange that they have persevered with Pinot noir at the Maipu site.

The company has been very successful in the market place with all their wines and at wine competitions, even in France where the Syrah topped the international competition. They probably have Argentina's best Sauvignon (blanc) and Riesling.

In keeping with their solid grasp of the future, the company is rebuilding sections of their showpiece Drummond winery to cater for expansion, also temperature-controlled storage for finished case goods.

Leaders in the Argentine market with their quality varietal wines under their premium Luigi Bosca label and blended wines behind the Señor del Robledal mark. Robledal means Arizu in the vasco language. The company now has many flourishing export markets, the biggest customer is Sweden followed by the U.K.

As one travels Argentina, it is apparent that the lesson of wine being made in the vineyard has seeped through to all corners of the country. Alberto Arizu, who heads the family company, has learnt this lesson well. He is indeed a lucky man having a wife and two sons who all work very hard with him to uphold this sound Arizu tradition.

73

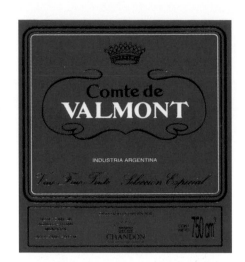

The winery buildings of Chandon

Offices and entertainment facilty

CHANDON

As part of the enormous international Louis - Vuiton - Moet - Hennessy group, Chandon are better known in the wine world as an off-shoot of the French champagne house, Moet & Chandon. It is Moet's policy to globalize and they have developed satellites in eight countries. With their 1959 arrival in Argentina most people felt that this was a major breakthrough and, based on the company's performance in other countries, that they would be a leader in wine quality

Yet, this does not seem to be the criterion; making enormous amounts of money in a sparkling wine thirsty-market was, in fact, the bottom line. Chandon, with its three sparkling labels, dominates more than 50 percent of the local bubbly market with an inferior, lowest-common-denominator Chandon label using mainly the charmat (bulk tank) production method. This is outlawed in their Champagne homeland. On several visits to the Agrelo bodega, the quality of the sparkling wine offered, as representative of their efforts, I have found to be bitterly disappointing.

It is a different story with their two still, varietal wine labels. The Paul Galard Malbec and Renaud Poirier Chardonnay, especially, would be among the country's better wines.

All this seems incongruous as the company is really on top of the wine business; they have vineyards in the best locations, technical expertise and a fine bodega. The reader may well ask, who am I to question one of the world's premier wine houses - a good question?

Chandon has superb vineyards located in key regions. In the lower Mendoza River areas there are 130 ha of Chardonnay, Pinot noir, Semillon, Sauvignon (blanc), Malbec, the two Cabernets, Petit Verdot and Mouvedre. In the high river areas of Lujan there is another fruit salad mix of 142 ha including Chardonnay, Chenin, Pinot blanc and Semillon whites, while the reds are interestingly Cabernet Franc, Malbec, Merlot, the two Pinots - Meunier and noir. In Tupungato there are currently 40 ha of Chardonnay, Merlot and Pinot noir. The company intends to bring their total plantings to 500 ha by the turn of the century.

RED WINE

ETCHART

MENDOZA

MALBEC

1993

PRODUCT
OF ARGENTINA
ELABORADO Y FRACCIONADO
POR ARNALDO ETCHART S.A.
13% ALC/VOL

EMBOTELLADO
EN ORIGEN
PROCEDENCIA MENDOZA
MENDOZA
ARGENTINA 750 ML

Author's Choice

Malbec is a good buy

ETCHART

In 1938, Arnaldo Etchart purchased a Cafayate, Salta vineyard, La Florida, and winery that dated back to the 1850s. He became so famous through the Cafayate Torrontés that he acquired another property in Lujan de Cuyo, Mendoza province. During 1992 he merged with the marketing company, Cuisenir Argentina, a division of the French drinks giant, Pernod Rickard, who also own the famed Australian Orlando wine company, makers of Jacob's Creek wines.

The holdings were subsequently purchased by the French company which meant an immediate injection of much needed capital to modernize the two plants and extensive vineyards.

Being the only winery situated on RN 40, 22 km south of Mendoza at Perdriel, Etchart enjoys a dominant position. The workers in this see-through winery have a spectacular view of the Andes.

By comparison with the Etchart holdings of over 250 ha in Salta province, this Mendoza property is small with, currently, only 50 ha. The winery is concentrating on red varietals Malbec, Merlot and Cabernet Sauvignon; the whites are Chardonnay and Chenin. These are good, sound commercial wines that will not disappoint. The company buys-in grapes and wine from third parties who meet their criteria.

It is surprising that so many companies, and Etchart Lujan is one, have no aspirations of making a truly great wine. Etchart has very savvy viticulturists, good vineyards, excellent winery facilities that are capable of the task — and dedicated winemakers — yet, like so many others they are playing the lower end of the market only. Probably that is where the money is?

One would hope that as a challenge to the winemakers, and for Argentina, one day soon these resources will be directed to an Argentine classic — red or white wine.

Already the Etchardt wines have broad overseas markets with Europe (UK and Holland being dominant) taking 71% of exports, South and North America each taking 13% and Asia nearly 2%.

Lagarde vineyard at Lujan de Cuyo

Author's Choice

Viognier

LAGARDE

Lagarde is a fascinating winery. Over its first century of operations the company has developed a strong reputation for providing limited quantity varietal wines to the Argentine restaurant trade. One of their wines, the excellent but unpopular varietal, Semillon, is Argentina's oldest mark having been constantly on the market since 1942. Today, they are the first winery in South America to introduce the excellent varietal, Viognier, a wine which should become an Argentine standard.

Many other things are fascinating about Lagarde, including its century old bodega comprising three attached buildings which cater for winemaking, bottling and storage. Situated in the Drummond portion of Lujan de Cuyo, the bodega and entertainment area are located in a shady grove of assorted trees. These slate-floored adobe buildings breathe the roots of country, family winemaking. With the recent acquisition by the strong conglomerate Impsa, headed by the Pescarmona family, one can foresee some major changes. Firstly, the family has a hands-on desire, and one would think a 21st century approach

to marketing outside the country. It would be reasonable to expect production to be doubled in a short time to cater for the vast North American market, where a leading distributor has been appointed.

The product range is also fascinating. A blanc de noir made from Pinot noir and Malbec has attracted favorable comment and the Champagne Lagarde is arguably the best packaged wine in the country; has good flavor also! The range of varietals includes a multi-award winning Syrah — Lujan is a top place to grow Syrah — and the standards Cabernet, Malbec, Merlot and a pleasing blended Crianza made from the combined varietals. Crianza is a Spanish term indicating that the wine is not released for sale before three years and has spent (in Rioja) at least 12 months in 225 litre oak casks.

Other than the Viognier, Lagarde has the compulsory Chardonnay and Sauvignon (blanc) in its white wine portfolio. This is a company worth watching as their products become available in English-speaking countries.

Carlos Tizio-Mayer

Author's Choice

Norton Privada

Vineyards:

High Agrelo: Chardonnay, Chenin, Riesling, Sauvignon, Semillon, Barbera, Cabernet S., Malbec, Merlot, Sangiovese, Syrah,

Agrelo: 30 ha Merlot,

Perdriel: 100 ha Cabernet Sauvignon

Lujan de Cuyo; 20 ha Malbec, Merlot, Cab. Sauvignon

Medrano: Chardonnay, Sangiovese

Domestic labels:

Norton Cosecha Tardia, Norton Viñedo Perdriel Red, Dalton

Norton Champagne, Norton Brut, Viñedo Perdriel White

Export labels:

Norton - Barbera, Malbec, Merlot, Perdriel, Privada, Sangiovese

Norton Chardonnay.

NORTON

A British civil engineer working on the Trans Andes railway, Edmund James Palmer Norton, left an indelible mark on Argentine wine, Bodegas Norton. In partnership with Grant Dalton, he bought land in Perdriel, Lujan de Cuyo, and established one of the early Argentine wineries. Whereas Dalton returned to England, Norton married a local lady, Juana Suárez, and nurtured the development of the winery.

Norton's previous railway company association meant that he was able to negotiate a deal whereby only Norton wines were served in the trains' dining rooms. This was grand exposure and made Norton wines a household word among the traveling public.

Being first to establish south of the Mendoza River, Norton did not know that his choice of vineyard sites would set the future standard for Argentine fine wine. In terms of grape quality, the vineyards located in Perdriel, Agrelo and Lujan are three of the nation's best sites for fine wine styles.

In 1956 the company was sold to Manuel Santos. Eventually it passed to his sons Ricardo and Alberto, Ricardo being the man on the spot. In one sense, it was sad that disputes between the pair eventually forced a sale in 1989. From personal experience I know of the creative work that Ricardo was applying to the progress of this fine bodega. He was among the first to understand that new ideas were necessary for an ailing industry. He brought in skilled California winemaking consultant, Steve Rasmussen, and had started to make giant steps forward when the decision was made to sell the bodega.

Austrian business man and glassmaker, Gernot Langes-Swarovski, purchased the winery in 1989 and installed son Michael to lead the rather drastic changes that were to be made. One of their major decisions was to employ INTA grape researcher and California-trained viticulturist, Carlos Tizio-Mayer, as technical manager. Carlos Tizio brought enormous energy, ebullience and experience to the operation.

The surgery has been all-embracing - new vineyards with new trellises and a renewed and extended winery with the latest technology from around the world. There can be no doubt that all this has changed the wine to more modern upmarket styles. Still, every Thursday people come from far and wide, walking, riding a cycle, or in luxury cars to purchase their demijohns of house red.

Norton is, without doubt, a very professional organization producing excellent wines. Their reds have always been personal favorites, the Privada (Private) an outstanding blend of Cabernet, Merlot and Malbec. The high quality of the excellent Medrano Chardonnay and the Norton Brut is surprising.

Adriano Senetiner with tomorrow's grape picker

Author's Choice

Cadus Malbec

A breathtaking, winter's morning scene at Villa Blanca - sunrise in the east, Andes in the west.

82

NIETO & SENETINER

Best known for their local brand of Santa Isabel, Nieto & Sentiner have burst onto the international market with the Vistalba Valley and Casa Nieto & Senetiner labels. Founded in 1969 by Nicanor Nieto and Adriano Senetiner, the company has established separate wineries in Carrodilla for the Santa Isabel label and in Vistalba for the excellent range of flagship Cada and Vistalba Valley wines.

The Carrodilla winery, home of the Santa Isabel label, in addition to the very latest equipment, has a storage capacity of 5.5 million litres; the Vistalba winery can handle two million litres of fine wine. Under the direction of the surviving partner, Adriano Senetiner, and a technical team lead by Walter Brescia, a dedicated professional, there is a constant on-going search for excellence. The Casa wines have been extremely successful in wine contests, more so in prestigious Italian and French wine competitions.

As the technical team gains further experience working with new oak and the top varieties such as Syrah, Malbec and Cabernet, this label will become a household name throughout the wine world. This knowledge will be expedited when their focus is moved to southern hemisphere practices.

Maybe it smacks of romantics, but few wines are made in a more pleasant and scenic atmosphere. The interpretation of Vistalba is "morning view", referring to the view of the nearby Andes in morning light - a sight never to be forgotten. The winery is surrounded by an arboral fiesta. The driveway is lined with productive olive trees and the landscaped grounds feature clearly-signed trees from every continent. A traditional Argentine barbecue, swimming pool and tennis courts add a homely touch to this magnificent Villa Blanca.

Production is now edging up to 900,000 cases annually, exports now being 10 percent of this amount. This will increase dramatically as the world learns about the quality of these wines and is prepared to pay a reasonable price for them. Their three top reds Cabernet, Syrah and Malbec certainly equal the best of Argentina and, if one can take notice of international judgments, they rank with the best in the world. The Barbera and Merlot wines will also find a following among aficionados of these varieties.

With 250 ha of their own vineyards in Lujan de Cuyo and Tupungato the two wineries have access to the best fruit in the country; a sure road to success if properly vinified.

FABRE MONTMAYOU

Hervé Joyaux Fabre and Arnaud Meillan

When a bordelais moves to any place on earth, whether it be Australia, Argentina, Chile, he will surely make Bordeaux wine; simply, because that's what he knows. However, those who wander south of the Equator usually add the Burgundian Chardonnay to their repertoire, and that is exactly what this small group from Bordeaux have done at Domaine Vistalba.

It is strange to hear bordelaise wax eloquently about the vineyard land in other countries, yet this group claim that Vistalba is the absolute tops. That makes them pretty smart judges!

Their 47 ha of vineyards contain Malbec, Cabernet Sauvignon, Chardonnay - and, surprisingly, Syrah. The Malbec vines are 50 years old and the balance are all 20 years plus. No herbicides or chemical fertilizers are used. Merlot is brought hundreds of kilometres from Rio Negro in the south. Once you visit this Vistalba property with its glorious views of the Andes,

you just have to believe that it would be impossible not to make really great wine in this locale.

It is a strange phenomenon that local wine critics have come down hard on the work of winemaker, Arnaud Meillan, yet these are clearly world-class wines. The Grand Vins, based on Malbec, is a star. More than 60 percent of wine goes to Asia, Germany and the USA while the balance goes into the large Buenos Aires market. They will be making their French debut soon.

84

WEINERT

After 40 years traveling the world and looking at wineries, it is almost a punishment for a writer to be shown over one more winery. One only needs to look through the winery door to obtain a clear picture of what is happening inside. Such were my thoughts upon arrival at Weinert. Following a tongue-lashing for being late for an appointment that I knew nothing about, the party was invited to tour the winery. For the above reasons and the old-fashioned type of winery that Weinert is, we politely, and eventually firmly, declined the invitation. They were extremely proud of the rows of large, old casks; a sign not accepted by most.

What followed was definitely a first; the winemaker cried — and her associate told us, "if you want to see a stainless steel winery you should go down the road to some other place." We took their advice on the first offering.

If you like their wine style, as many do, including the USAs #1 wine critic, then Weinert makes very good wines which bring top prices. These love/hate wines have a very definite place in the market for what could be classified as 19th century colonial wines. They are fully matured, and often over-matured in the large old casks, at the winery before sale. Today, as a general rule, the market demands younger and livelier wines with more fresh fruit; wines that feature the vineyard rather than the bodega.

The winery is named after the founder, Brazilian Bernardo Weinert, who in 1976 took as a partner one of Argentina's most respected winemakers, Raúl de la Mota. Nothing much changed over the next 20 years. The fermentation tanks are expoxy-lined concrete and are ideal for these wine styles.

From vineyards in Lujan and Tupungato, Weinert, now minus Sr. de la Mota, makes mainly red varietal wine and a varietal Chardonnay. The red wine varietals include Cabernet Sauvignon, Malbec and Merlot and these are blended for the generic range of Cavas de Weinert and Carrascal. There is a blended Carrascal white made from a Semillon and Sauvignon (blanc), while the Montfleury Rosé is a blend of Cabernet and Malbec.

85

INTA

In many ways, the National Institute of Agricultural Technology (INTA), is the central focus in Argentine wine.

Both Silvia Avagnania de Del Monte and Carlos Catania have worked together for 20 years to resolve Argentine viti-viniculturists many problems. Their work is all-encompassing, from entertaining hundreds of international visitors to authoring an equal number of publications on subjects from downy mildew fungicides to agroecological zoning of grape varieties.

Silvia began her pioneering work at INTA in 1971, while Carlos was an agronomist graduate of the University de Cuyo who subsequently went onto further studies in Montpellier, France.

In the 1970s their first task was to sort-out the mess of varieties in the vineyards. Grapes had come from everywhere and had good, bad and indifferent names. They identified and classified hundreds of European varieties, and clones, which always appear in new vineyard areas.

Based in Lujan de Cuyo their research, development and extension work encompasses wine regions nationwide. Their studies include virus-free multiplication of all the the major grape varieties, canopy management and trellising studies, soil management, irrigation and much more.

All field trials are made into wine and evaluated in the Centre's own mini-winery, and then they actually sell the fruits of their labor — good wine, good buying if you can get to Mendoza! Both Silvia and Carlos are professors at the annual sensory evaluation course run by the center. It would be impossible to stress the value of the great work that this universally-loved, remarkable pair have achieved.

A MAN AND HIS CAMERA

Augusto Foix

When growing up, children often have problems in deciding what they desire to be in life. At 12 years of age, Augusto Foix didn't know whether he wanted to be a photographer or a winemaker. He had been born to a third generation family of winemakers and already had his own darkroom in a corner of the bodega.

When decision time arrived, Argentine wine was in a downturn and he chose the best of both worlds - to become a photographer specializing in wine subjects. Augusto subsequently became a publisher and, arguably, South America's leading wine photographer. His superb book *"Mendoza - A Land of Sun and Wine"* is a classic in photography and the publishers art. Also he publishes Del Vino Professional.

On hearing of an event where the author's computer, manuscript, videos, cameras and photographs were all stolen, Augusto spontaneously offered all the photos necessary to finish this work. His work fills these pages from cover to cover - any unworthy photos are those of the author.

87

THE FOREIGNERS

In a land of foreigners the new invasion of wine people is more broadly based than the originals; the new lot come from around the world. This interesting mix can be classified into three groups:

The first would be those who buy land, buildings and vineyards and make wine under their own labels. Numbered among these are neighbors from Chile who, having developed strong export markets with their home-grown product, realize the great potential of Argentina. A strange mix of people from Austria, California, Denmark, France and Germany are others who have also invested heavily in this awakening giant.

Unlike the locals, the foreigners realize how many jewels there are in the Argentine vinous crown. One example would be land which although increasing in price rapidly, is cheap by standards in any other top wine growing nation. With years of experience in the markets of the world, the foreigners know exactly which wines, and how many, these markets require. Rightly or wrongly, they can see big profits in the short term. Still, they are taking a stake in the country, and the myriad risks that go with doing business in Argentina.

The second group would be the so-called flying winemakers who base themselves at a local winery, buy in grapes or wine, and make Argentine wines to be sold under their own or other labels.

A third interesting group is another type of flying winemaker who produce what is known in the trade as buyers own brand (B.O.B). This is a specialty of the large UK supermarket chains who will buy something like 50,000 cases of popular varietals using a contracted winery premises and wine - made under their winemaker's supervision. One giant UK group employs Portuguese-based Australian, Peter Bright, to make large quantities at Trapiche to be sold under their own label.

In the first group there are many famous names setting-up shop in Argentina. Joining the list of champagne makers mentioned elsewhere are two notable Chilean companies Concha y Toro and Santa Carolina who have both purchased existing Argentina wineries

Austrian businessman, Gernot Langes-Swarovski, has made a significant investment and under his son Michael's guidance, thoroughly changed the face of old-timer Norton. Together, this family combination with the help of some very competent professionals, have effectively brought a new dimension to Argentine wine quality, more details on page 81.

Winelovers in the USA will closely follow the fortunes of Kendall Jackson who is making a most positive wine statement in both Chile and Argentina. Unlike other newcomers, Kendall Jackson has opted to buy land and grapes in the very cool regions in both countries. Their first wines under their Argentine Mariposa label wines attest to the wisdom of this quality decision which, by Argentine standards, comes at an upmarket price.

Achieving the loftiest goals for owner Jess Jackson at Vinas de Tupungato are two bright and young people from California. Before joining the Kendall Jackson empire, Greg Adams had spent five years as a freelance viticultural consultant in Mendoza and had the requisite local knowledge to provide answers for any newcomer. KJ realized this and gave him the task of purchasing a tract of virgin desert and turning it into a profitable vineyard.

Two properties have been purchased; one of 400 ha in Ugarteche which is the winery site, and another 1,000 ha in Tupungato. The towering Mt Tupungato, second highest peak in the western hemisphere, looks down on the property which has been planted with Cabernet, Malbec, Merlot and Chardonnay vines from California. An on-site nursery has been established and will provide vines for further plantings at both sites.

Pinot noir specialist winemaker, Lynda Hanson, arrived via a different route. Finishing work in California on a Friday, she immediately boarded a plane bound for Mendoza, arrived on Saturday morning and went straight to work making her first vintage in 1997.

Kendall Jackson or more correctly, Mariposa, the chosen name for the brand, will feature Malbec as its uppermost

wine in the USA. Not a hard job for winemaker Lynda who came to Argentina as a Pinot noir devotee but to use her own words, fell in love with Malbec.

In the town of Tunuyan is the bodega of an interesting character, Heinrich Vollmer, whose home base is at Ellerstadt in Germany's Rheinpfalz region. His home weingut appears to provide sufficient funding for this enthusiastic adventure-seeker to wander the world climbing mountains alone - an obsession that nearly came to an end in the Andes. Vollmer fell during an earthquake there and broke a leg.

He was eventually carried 70 km to safety by a group of local Indians. So grateful for this mercy, in 1987 Vollmer established a bodega in Tunuyan that now employs nine families of his life saving friends.

Unfortunately, when I visited his wineries in both Germany and Argentina to authenticate this story first-hand, he was somewhere else in the world, not necessarily climbing mountains.

Among other well-known European names are Spain's Marques de Grignon, (Don Carlos Falco) from Toledo who produces excellent wines at the Norton facility in Lujan de Cuyo. The Marques is a most engaging man who, in his earlier years, studied agricultural engineering in both Belgium and California. The latter experience influenced him to pioneer the planting of the French varieties Cabernet Sauvignon and Merlot in his native Spain, varieties that were later followed by Syrah, Petit Verdot and Chardonnay. In addition to being a skilled winemaker, very few of his craft live in the family's 12th century residence! The Marques de Grignon wines are bound for the European market, Spain in particular.

Making a profound quality statement using grapes from the warmer east Mendoza region are the brothers Jacques and Francois Lurton from Bordeaux, France. Using the winemaking facilities of Bodegas Escorihuela, it is fair to say that they have set a quality standard that locals would be wise to follow if they want to compete in the "fighting varietal" category. All their Mendoza wines Malbec, Tempranillo, Chardonnay, Chenin, and Pinot gris — are surprisingly good wines. The Pinot gris is a personal favorite.

The most interesting thing about the Lurtons is that not only do they make wines in Eastern Europe, France and Argentina but also Australia, Chile and Spain! By using itinerant winemakers, they are in the unique situation of making at least three vintages every year in both Northern and Southern Hemispheres - that has to be some sort of a record? From their ageing chateau in a small Bordeaux village these multi-language entrepreneurs are setting many new standards for international wine at affordable prices. Their wines have an extensive global market.

These newcomers are doing much for their adopted country by putting their immediate stamp of approval, i.e. their reputation, on the quality and potential of Argentine wine. This would have taken the locals more than a decade to achieve on their own.

One giant UK supermarket group employs Portuguese-based Australian, Peter Bright, to make large quantities of wine at Trapiche to be sold under their own label.

Norton's chief, Austrian, Michael Halstrick

A selection of labels from California, German, French and Spanish producers.

The magnificence of Tupungato scenery

Trucks laden with grapes roar through Tupungato, day and night, in harvest period

92

UCO VALLEY

Heading south along the RN40 from Mendoza, take a right turn onto the RP86 at Ugarteche, then after a total of 72 km the wine traveller will arrive at the attractive village of Tupungato. The town is probably the furthest west into the cordillera and located at altitude 1100 metres. Tupungato, unquestionably is the centre of one of the world's great viticultural areas.

The town has but two registered wineries; the well-established Giaquinta brothers a little east in the village of La Arboleda and Alfrans in the village of El Paral. The Giaquinta family have been a force in the area since 1915 when they established their vineyard. Like so many others, back in 1968 Giaquinta started selling wine in bulk and then with the coming of the second generation they moved into fine wines. Since 1993 the brothers have made a varietal Chardonnay and moved into 750 ml bottles as well as litre bottles and demijohns. Obviously their Malbec is a top wine as Mariposa purchased some for their first bottling of Tapestry.

As yet, it is not the wineries themselves that have or will make Uco Valley's fame, rather the myriad vineyards scattered all over the area. When you see such names as Catena, Chandon, La Rural, Mariposa, Nieto y Senetiner and Trapiche with big holdings in the area, you know well that this is pay dirt. Due to the very sloping nature of the terrain, very little of this Valley is irrigated by the conventional furrow watering, and because of this water situation, land was relatively cheap. The cost of bores, pumps, power, irrigation systems and the need for grafted vines dramatically boosts the establishment costs of a vineyard in the region.

The region will ripen all varieties with tremendous fruit flavors at a later date than at lower levels. Wine flavor is all about hang-time, the almost delayed, slow-ripening of the fruit. This can only happen in a cool season, or at a lower latitude or higher level.

In Mendoza province, Tupungato offers three of these possibilities, a higher level, slow-ripening and long hang time. Yet, with careful application of varieties, other Mendoza districts can, and have, reached the highest levels of quality with different varieties.

93

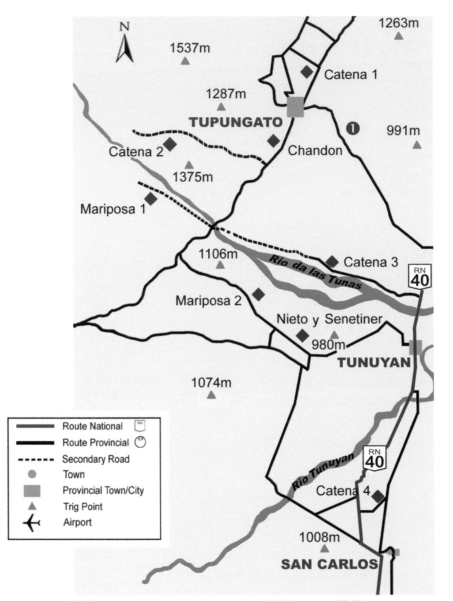

VINEYARDS OF UCO VALLEY

Position: 33.00'S 68.20'W

Bodegas of Uco Valley	Address	Town
San Polo SA	San Martin	San Carlos
Coop La Consulta	San Martin 640	San Carlos
Francisco Hnos	San Martin 1962	Tunuyan
Silvestre Hnos	San Martin 1942	Tunuyan
Heinrich Vollmer	Casilla de Correo 65	Tunuyan
Giaquinta Hnos #1	Carril Zapata s/n	Tupungato
Alfran SA	La Gloria	Tupungato

AWESOME ARGENTINA

Kendall Jackson (Mariposa) vineyard, Tupungato

Desert country in the foreground, gives way to the pre-cordillera and then Mt. Tupungato

95

San Rafael Wine and Leisure Country.

San Rafael

Situated 230 kms south of the capital Mendoza, San Rafael is an important oasis for reasons other than wine. It is an extremely attractive regional capital (population 165,000) with its own identity and engaging tourist attractions. Shady trees are very much part of San Rafael, providing comfort and beauty in the hot summers. The tree-lined streets somehow reflect the wonderful nature of San Rafael's people.

If you speak Italian, you can live here without ever knowing a word of Español. Italian culture, language and names are prominent in the region. Yet it was the French who were the first group of settlers in the region shortly after 1879 when General Roca's Indian War (Campaña del Desierto) made the land safe for settlement. This was at a time of mass immigration to Argentina and the new settlers brought skills and money to this frontier region. In particular, the French brought advanced viticultural skills and new grape varieties.

Swiss immigrants Otto and Ana Suter were one of the first fully fledged winemaking couples to arrive in 1897, being attracted by a Swiss settlement in the region. The arrival of the railroad in 1903 saw the colony extended out as far as 25 de Mayo and San Rafael had an assured future of steady growth.

San Rafael went through a difficult period in the 1970s and the mid '80s when wine production in the north assumed oceanic proportions; discounting was the order of the day. At the same time, domestic consumption dropped by 50 percent. San Rafael producers floundered; the economy almost collapsed. It was then realized that they had to broaden the city's economic base.

They chose the only tool that cost nothing — tourism. What the city has achieved in the past decade is absolutely amazing. Today the district has many well-promoted tourist destinations and an effective, friendly and well-staffed tourist center.

Other than an attractive, clean and friendly city, the region offers three quite varied and spectacular tourist circuits. In less than two hours the visitor can be horse-riding in the Andes or in the snow country at El Sosneado near the Chilean border. The other two routes take in the white water sports, fishing and many dams, including Grand Valley, to the south and west of San Rafael. The long-nosed winelover should not overlook the numerous splendid wineries!

Valentin Bianchi runs its large international operation from San Rafael, all other prominent wineries have their administration and marketing offices in Buenos Aires. Yet, Bianchi is one of the nation's most efficient firms and a long-time, large exporter. In fact, it was Bianchi who introduced the writer to

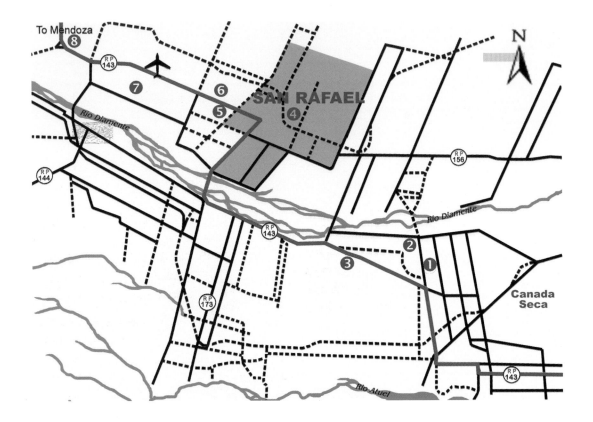

WINERIES OF SAN RAFAEL

Position: 34.40 S 68.33 W

	Bodega	Address	District
1	Lavaque	Ruta Prov 165 s/n	Cañada Seca
2	Barral y Roca	Ruta Provincial 165	Cañada Seca
3	Simonassi Lyon	Ruta 143	Rama Caida
4	Valentin Bianchi	Torres 500	San Rafael
5	Jean Rivier	Ruta 143	San Rafael
6	Suter SA	Ruta 143 s/n	Las Paredes
7	Balbi Vineyard	Jensen y Sarmiento	Las Paredes
8	V. Bianchi (Sparkling)	Ruta 143 s/n	Las Paredes

BALBI

In 1930, Juan Balbi founded the bodega that now bears his name. In some very distant office, somewhere in the world, the international wine and spirits giant Allied-Domecq decided to purchase this solid San Rafael winery in 1992. Obviously Balbi was a good business with a good name. The giant could pump a steady flow of cash into the winery and vineyards and make it a viable, progressive partner in its international holdings.

Located at Las Paredes five kilometres north of San Rafael, the Balbi winery has almost too many new winemaker toys. As is often the case in Argentina, old concrete tanks have been lined with epoxy resin and new stainless steel temperature-controlled tanks and rows of new oak casks have been added to much other new winery equipment. It is a very professional operation under the guiding hand of Pedro Yañez.

Balbi is a classic example of French Bordeaux winemaking wherever the Bordelaise go in the New World. Due to Balbi's affiliation with the well-known Calvet house, and being in opposite hemispheres, allows the French to oversee the vintage in Argentina during their off-season. Instead of trying to put the fruit of the San Rafael vineyard in the bottle, as a general rule, the intent is to make a Bordeaux style wine in Argentina. Maybe this tough, tannic style has a following among those who enjoy buying wines for ageing - but the general belief is that wine is made to drink rather than hide in a closet for years.

Current vintages certainly show a change in style including the use of new oak - and other very drinkable wines without oak. These wines are showing nice fruit sweetness, mainly due to Balbi's philosophy of purchasing grapes from the Uco Valley. This is probably the best fruit in the country, and blending it with local San Rafael grapes is a lesson that could be studied by other local producers.

The export range is a distinctive lot and among the normal run of Malbec, Cabernet, Chenin and Chardonnay varietals there is well-made sweetened 100% Syrah Rose - something different and pleasant. It is fair to say that Argentine winemakers are much happier making red wines than white, due mainly to an overwhelming local demand for red wines, a similar situation to Bordeaux. At this early time of development, this shows in the Balbi wines as they wrestle with Chenin from the Loire - and Chardonnay from Burgundy. As brand manager Carlos Fernandez shows these wines around the world and has consumer feedback, this writer has faith in Balbi's ability to come to grips with these two very different varieties.

At Bianchi a glistening hi-tech winery is augmented by a traditional tasting room.

Author's Choice

Malbec

Vineyards:
Finca Asti, Las Paredes: 100 ha
Chardonnay, Chenin, Riesling, Torrontés,
Bonarda, Cabernet Sauvignon, Malbec

Finca Las Paredes: Chardonnay,
Sauvignon, Riesling, Cabernet, pinot
noir,

Elsa's Vinyard, Rama Caída: 110 ha
Chardonnay, Chenin, Semillon, Cabernet,
Malbec, Merlot

VALENTIN *Bianchi* BIANCHI

BIANCHI
CHARDONNAY

SAN RAFAEL

DENOMINACION SAN RAFAEL CONTROLADA

VINO FINO BLANCO

Envasado en Origen · Procedencia Mendoza · San Rafael · Producido y Fraccionado
por Valentín Bianchi S.A.C.I.F. · Cte. Torres 500 · San Rafael · Mendoza
Establecimiento Nº K- 71831 · Distribuidores Seagram de Argentina S.A. · S. de
Bustamante 54 Bs. As. · Industria Argentina. I.N.V.S.R. Nº   Cont. Neto   **750 CM3**

VALENTIN BIANCHI

Bianchi could be classified as one of the rocks upon which San Rafael is built. Their administrative and main bodega facility is downtown on Torres Avenue, and the new sparkling facility is the first visible sight one sees of San Rafael on the main road eight km from town. Over the years, the Bianchi family has been a tireless and generous promoters of all things about San Rafael.

Although not one of the earliest players in the region (1928), like many Italian families Bianchi has developed a strong family base with relatives controlling every department of the company's activities. New, outside, professional blood in the executive ranks would bring new thinking to some of the wine styles and the company's management. Bianchi can, and should, be one of Argentina's top four producers.

The new sparkling facility on Highway 143 is as modern and technologically advanced as most in the world. This facility has given the company a chance to show what they can do and, no doubt, they are producing superb sparkling wines.

At the other end of the spectrum, Bianchi has produced Argentina's most exciting entry level wine called

New Age. This semi-sweet, fruity and flowery wine is exactly the style that will attract generation X and lead them on to more sophisticated wines.

For many years the company has made their claim to export fame with the two excellent Argentine standards - Malbec and Chenin - varieties that seem to thrive in San Rafael. The current crop of these standards is better than ever. The Malbec is outstanding. Whether it is the magnet of export market mania or for other reasons, Bianchi has taken to the Cabernet/Chardonnay route with considerable success. The company has 350 ha of vines divided between three different vineyards in varying locations. These produce 70-80% of their requirements and each provides individual wines. All export wines come from these vineyards rather than contracted growers.

One can only compliment any company on moving towards chemical-free, sustainable agriculture in their vineyards. Like other progressive viticulturists in Argentina, Bianchi has first done this in its principal Elsa's Vineyard in Rama Caída.

The company realizes the value of tourism and tours and sales are available Monday - Friday at their downtown facility.

103

Bodegas Lavaque, a landmark in Cañada Seca.

Lavaque's impressive new barrel room.

Author's Choice
Chardonnay

104

LAVAQUE

Located 13 km south of San Rafael city is Cañada Seca is the impressive Spanish-style bodega of Lavaque; very gracious hosts. Driving through this unpopulated farm area the sight of this impressive all-white building is something of a shock, as is also the inside of the bodega. Spotlessly clean and orderly, it is a credit to winemaster Claudio Sosa.

While the look of this traditional winery — with rows of large old carved, ornamental oak vats — prepares one for the individual wines of Lavaque, there are some surprises in store for the visitor. Not the least of these are the white wine blend of French Chardonnay with the Italian grape Ugni blanc, an interesting method of keeping the price of the French classic grape at an affordable level.

Lavaque, who are important players in the domestic market, use only grapes from their own estates for their large range of wines. At this time exports include Cabernet Sauvignon-Merlot, Malbec and the Chardonnay-Ugni blanc. A new range of medium-priced red and white blends have also been included in the export portfolio.

The company's limited top range is Felix Lavaque and this includes Cabernet, Pinot noir and Chardonnay.

In line with the dynamic, progressive nature of the Lavaque corporation, (they purchased the Cafayate bodega Michel Torino in 1993), expansion is taking place in both the winery and vineyards. A new bottling line and the rows of new oak barrels add to the winery as a showpiece of wine quality and efficiency. The 165 ha of vineyards are a similar story in professionalism. There are further plantings of all the popular varietals with Chardonnay emerging as a potential star.

Chardonnay and Pinot noir are relatively recent developments in the New World. During this period of development Argentina was, in a sense, locked out of the world's fast-moving technological progress in viticulture and winemaking; with these two grapes in particular.

The catching-up period will be lengthy and difficult, but Lavaque, with all its tools, is giving it a good shot. It is encouraging that Lavaque understands the benefits of study in foreign lands for their viti-vinicultural teams who visited and studied in California recently.

The initial cost of minimizing the nearly annual hail-stone havoc in the vineyards is about $7,000 per hectare. At this stage 60 hectares have been netted; a positive commitment that is continuing. This typifies the Lavaque approach which is also evident in their extensive northern holdings.

Lookout, Villa Traful

106

SUTER

Bearing in mind the natural beauty and wealth of their own country, as a general rule the Swiss are not a migrating race of people - they are content with their lot at home. Therefore, it was something of a surprise when Otto Suter and his wife Ana appeared at the Indian frontier town of San Rafael near the end of the 19th century. Initially they had considered Mendoza as a destination but the lure of wilder parts saw them board their horse and cart for the 230 km trip south with their belongings.

The original Suter vineyard was probably the first established in South America using the Riesling variety. To this day, Riesling is still used in a blend with Chenin for their Fritzwein. The Suter family, grapegrowers at heart, has developed an extensive vineyard network in the San Rafael region providing them with adequate supplies of fine grapes.

The company already has 220 ha of vines and this amount increases by about 10 percent annually. The six vineyards are located in the familiar areas of Cañada Seca, Las Paredes and El Cerrito. From their own nurseries they produce about 70,000 young vines annually from selected mother vines.

It is interesting to see two Pinots, blanc and gris, among their stocks. Planted in the right regions and carefully vinified, these are potentially two of Argentina's great white wines in a world that is awash with Chardonnay.

The winery is the classic style of old-fashioned thinking — clean as a whistle, and a show place of large old oak casks which, for tourists, conjure-up all the good things and magic of wine. Yet, other than these cosmetic uses they, sadly, have little purpose in today's modern winemaking process. Temperature-controlled stainless steel has been the way to go for the past 50 years.

Three brothers of the fourth generation, headed by Alberto in Buenos Aires; Daniel is the winemaker and Carlos the winery director. It is interesting that a leading company in almost any country can survive for 90 years without a Cabernet in the company line-up, a clear indication of how dependent they have been on their well-accepted white wines and Malbec.

For the first *JS* Cabernet Sauvignon fruit was chosen from their Santa Carolina vineyard at El Cerrito. This wine has received enthusiastic support in the Argentine market and is slowly being introduced to international markets. This will improve as the marketing specialists of Allied Domecq have taken over all major distribution.

AWESOME ARGENTINA

Patagonia landscape

Rio Negro Province

When visiting Rio Negro via the regional airport in neighboring Neuquen province, one has the feeling of arriving in another country. This is the start of Patagonia - and the South Pole. It surely is fascinating country! One only needs to cross the mighty Colorado River which flows from the Andes to the Atlantic and drive for 30 minutes to experience the vast deserted plains and plateau desert country.

Although the region has 41 wineries, again there is the anomalous situation where only one is selling on national and international markets.

At heart, these people are fruit growers producing some of the finest apples, stone fruit and table grapes to be found anywhere; wine grapes and winemaking are not a principal source of income. Neither the dedicated effort, nor money nor skills has, as yet, been applied to the right varieties which are probably Pinots blanc, gris and noir. It is easy to predict that stun-

ning white wines will come from this area; Chardonnay, the white and grey Pinots, Semillon, Sauvignon to a lesser extent. Possibly Viognier and the more exotic white hybrids such as Vignoles and Seyval could be real hits of the future.

It should not be long before many good producers in other provinces realize that it is here in Rio Negro, and possibly Neuquen, that outstanding grapes will be grown for Argentina's great wines of the future. Of course there are excellent sites in all other provinces, but the potential for making truly great wines is undoubtedly here in the cool south. While Cabernet is grown here, it could be a misfit.

Argentina is a country that suffers with frosts right across the country, but in most cases this is restricted to Spring and Autumn. Here in the south it can appear at almost anytime, even mid-summer, making it a major problem. Frost has a similar burning effect to fire; severe frost can be a wipe-out.

109

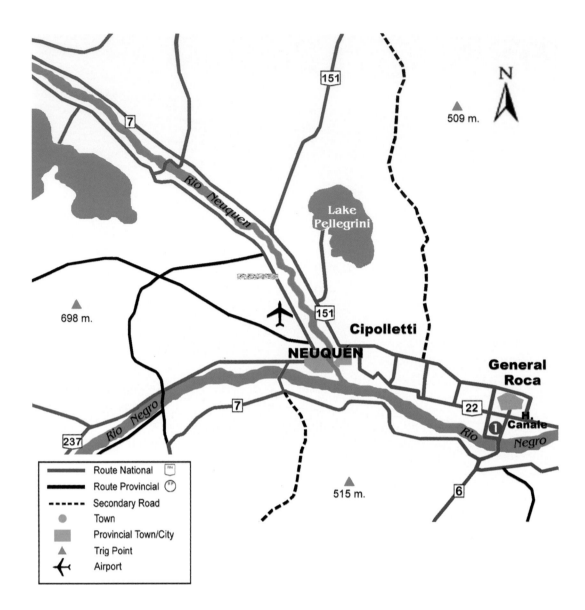

Nequen/RioNegro Regions

Position: 40.15S 68.15W

Bodega	Address	Town
1. Humberto Canale	Chacras 183	General Roca

HUMBERTO CANALE

The rapidly growing New Zealand regions of Alexandra and Queenstown are the world's most southerly commercial wine growing areas; Rio Negro/Neuquen are the next most southerly. The two regions on opposite sides of the Pacific Ocean have some similarities and also vast differences - and produce very different wine styles and types. The fear of annual devastating frost damage is the main similarity; frost can be equally as brutal as a fire raging through a vineyard.

The New Zealand regions are classic cold weather regions in the sense that they can only produce, on a regular basis, the German and northern France varieties such as Riesling, Pinot noir and Chardonnay; great stuff that is not in plentiful supply. The Rio Negro area has the warmer area Cabernets, Merlot and Semillon varieties as the backbone of their production. These varieties highlight the vast difference between the regions.

Although there are more than 9,000 ha planted to grapes, there are only a few producers in Argentina's northern Patagonia regions. Only Humberto Canale can be considered a national and international supplier. Founded in 1913, the Canale 550 ha fruit and grape farm is located eight km south of General Roca.

The 120 ha vineyards of the busy farm produces about 120,000 cases annually. There are three reds, Cabernet, Merlot and Pinot noir - and four whites - Chardonnay, Riesling, Semillon and Sauvignon. In addition to a vibrant domestic market which takes 75 percent of production, Canale wines are exported to Scandinavia, U.K., Germany, Switzerland, Austria and the USA.

At the time of publication, the winery was going through an almost complete refit with new stainless steel tanks, bottling line and other updates.

Nequen/Rio Negro is the "fruit bowl" of Argentina - and sometimes, the world. Canale is a major producer of apples, pears, plums, cherries, table grapes and peaches which find markets in Brazil, Germany and Scandinavia.

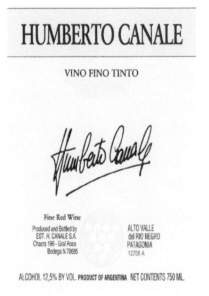

HUMBERTO CANALE

VINO FINO TINTO

Fine Red Wine

Produced and Bottled by
EST. H. CANALE S.A.
Chacra 186 - Gral Roca
Bodega N 70695

ALTO VALLE
del RIO NEGRO
PATAGONIA
12708 A

ALCOHOL 12,5% BY VOL. PRODUCT OF ARGENTINA NET CONTENTS 750 ML.

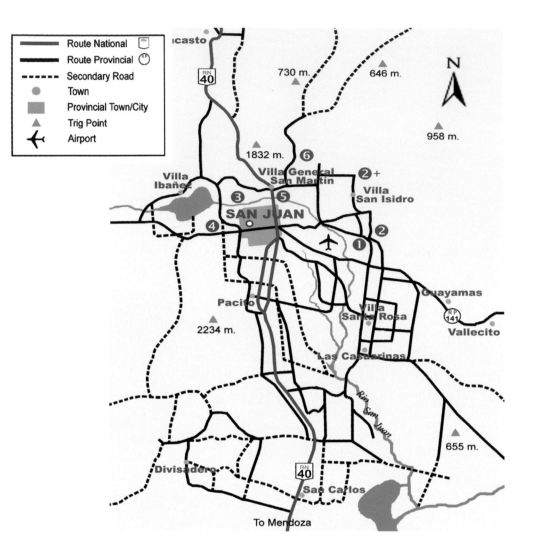

WINERIES OF SAN JUAN

Position: 31.00S 69.30W

1. Jose Borbore	Colon s/n	San Martin
2. Penaflor SA	Laprida s/n	San Martin
3. Graffigna	Colon 1342 N	Capital 5400
4. Saint Remy	San Martin 363 Oeste	Rivadavia
5. Santa Ana	Salta 667	Chimbas
6. Resero SA	Jachal y Blanco s/n	Santa Lucia

OTHER NOTABLE BODEGAS

Horacio Nesman	Salta 1600 Norte	Capital
Cinba	Jose de la Roza 2613	Capital
Los Parrales	Gnrl Acha 983 Norte	Capital
Jose A. Yanson	Enfermera Medina s/n	Caucete

SAN JUAN PROVINCE

The next oasis 170 km north of Mendoza is the capital of San Juan province, the source of much wine and 294 bodegas; yet only two who sell nationally. Of statistical interest to North Americans, this province produces more wine than the combined figures of the well-known California regions, Napa and Sonoma.

To produce this amount of fruit requires over 2,000 kms of irrigation channels within the boundaries of San Juan, a distance greater than from London to Bucharest, or Los Angeles to Seattle.

Having suffered unfairly in the shadow of Mendoza, San Juan is a rather poor province not really on the tourist route. The main route normally takes the northbound tourist further east to Cordoba, a major city rich with history.

Yet, San Juan de la Frontera is not without its own claims to fame. One of its sons, Domingo Faustino Sarmiento, became a famous author, scholar and, probably the most loved President. San Juan was also the place where a 49 year-old army officer, Juan Perón, first came to prominence following the 1944 earthquake devastation of the capital.

Perón was responsible for rebuilding San Juan. Two years later he became Argentina's president for the first time.

San Juan province has several major wine producing regions and these are widespread throughout the province,

from Jachal in the north to areas close to the city — and elevations varying from 650 - 1350 metres. There are three main valleys — Ullum, Tulum, and Zonda - all fed by the San Juan River. Nearest the capital is Tulum Valley, San Juan's highest producing region. Directly south is the Zonda wine region.

Another 20 kms further north east of Tulum, on the north side of the San Juan River, is the Ullum Valley. The province is a major provider of grapes and bulk wine to other provinces and many international buyers.

The reader is encouraged to closely follow the fortunes of El Perdenal, a potentially notable San Juan region in the pre-cordillera, as yet unknown to many. Situated directly west of Media Agua at 1,350 metres above sea level, early indications are that it will be a super-premium region for white varieties, Chardonnay, Sauvignon and Semillon. Mendocinos, jealous of its potential, will hasten to tell you that it is only 20 km inside the San Juan border.

An area of tourism interest is Jachal, closer to Villa Union, La Rioja, than any San Juan regions. In addition to wine and olives, Jachal is a region of artisan crafting, particularly 19th century loom weaving of ponchos and blankets.

As a measure of its viticultural strength, the province is big enough to have an enology school located in the capital.

113

Big toys for big boys at Borbore winery

114

BORBORE

The best of San Juan's wineries are equivalent to the general run of Mendoza's wineries but due mainly to isolation, are somewhat behind Mendoza's top ten producers. A dedicated and patient man in many ways, Juan Borbore is a leading figure in San Juan, Argentina's second largest producing province. He wants to slowly change San Juan's old ways.

For numerous reasons it would be grossly unfair to compare San Juan and Mendoza in any way. San Juan does not have the oil resources or an international highway as does Mendoza, which bring flocks of tourist dollars and other benefits. Among other reasons would be size; Mendoza's population is three times larger - geographically three times bigger - and because of this, more sophisticated. Yet a number of top Mendoza wineries have facilities in San Juan (Peñaflor, Catena, Santa Ana) - or draw grapes from their northern neighbor; sound business sense as almost everything is a lot cheaper in San Juan.

How and why does one change a winery when it has already been a successful exhibitor in a myriad of overseas competitions, would be a fair question? In this business a winery cannot stand still, they either goes forward or backwards - change is necessary to go forward. The obvious first step is to plant new vineyards in better growing regions - and in this desert climate. Borbore has achieved this in a unique way. He searched and found a desert forest area, where the natural tree growth was vigorous and healthy, and there successfully planted a vineyard. The unique feature of this vineyard is that it has the Pio de Palo range on the eastern side unlike southern vineyards which have the Andes to the west. This creates favorable wind currents bringing much needed cooling night-time breezes. The simple result - good fruit.

In the winery there has been considerable change with new buildings, new tank presses and adequate refrigeration - a much needed asset in these prevailing weather conditions. The result has been better wines which bring better returns in many ways. It has opened the door to exports, another learning process for this progressive winery.

The wines of Borbore are an interesting lot. The whites are clean and flavorsome with an excellent value Vino Blanco made with a mix of Chardonnay, Chenin, Ugni blanc and a delightful touch of Torrontes. The Cabernet Sauvignon is a surprisingly good wine for this region, yet it was the Malbec that surprised most of all; a really good wine — especially with the home cooked parillada we enjoyed with the reds.

The Borbore winery and its home vineyards, are located in San Martin department, 22 km east of the capital and is open to visitors by appointment only.

115

San Juan road signs

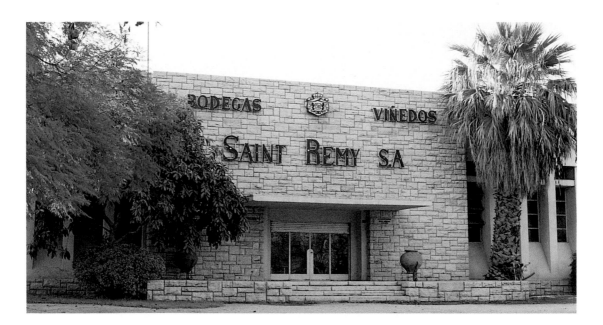

Bodegas Saint Remy, Avenue San Martin, Rivadavia, San Juan.

SAINT REMY

In a powerful statement, Saint Remy claims to have French government permission to use the word *Champagne* on their label. Be that as it may, sparkling wine production by the labor intensive methode champenoise (now called methode traditionalle) is a specialized business requiring specialized skills, equipment and grape sources to reach a reasonable standard. Making fizz with hot region grapes is fraught with all sorts of hazards - St. Remy seems to have satisfactorily overcome most of these problems in San Juan.

Using Chenin, Ugni blanc and Chardonnay grapes grown in San Martin department, and even a little Torrontes from their organic vineyard in Salta province, St. Remy has remarkably good juice for bubbly. These grapes are all harvested early in the season to maintain high natural acidity so necessary for producing good bubbles in the finished wine.

Currently all St. Remy wine is made by the classic hand-riddling method and in the quality arena is more than a worthy competitor for the locally based French champagne houses. But they do suffer in the market place from not having the merchandising muscle or expertise of the big boys. Their top label Duc de St. Remy (which originally came to Argentina from the land of legless frogs and cheese) is finely tuned with sweetness to the taste of the local market. I am assured that the very sweet Rosada is a favorite with the fairer sex.

Saint Remy is located close to the capital at 3267 Av. San Martin, Rivadavia, and has vineyards in San Martin department, Pio de Palo, and also at Cafayate in Salta province.

117

Pruning espalier (upright) vines, Pio de Palo vineyard, San Juan province

Overhead parral vines after pruning, Chilecito, La Rioja province

ANDEAN NORTH WEST

BOLIVIA

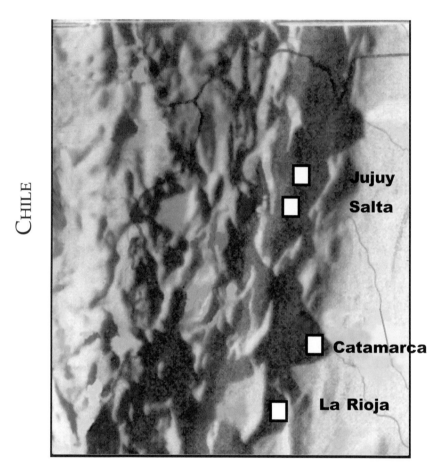

The three most northern provinces are Jujuy, Salta and Catamarca. All three share a western border with Chile; Jujuy also shares its northern border with Bolivia. La Rioja province is the buffer between the Cuyo and the northwest provinces.

Jujuy and Salta were among the first places settled by the Spanish invaders and enjoyed considerable good fortune as providers to the great mining ventures firstly in Bolivia to the north and later in Chile's Atacama desert to the west. High up in the Andes antiplano, Potosi, Bolivia was one of the world's richest silver mines, but it depended entirely on the outside world, particularly Argentina's north west, for everything except silver.

At that time, the north west was closer to the Lima, Peru centre of Spanish power; Buenos Aires was then considered a backwoods. Catamarca was not established until 1663, nearly a century after its neighbors. As power moved to Buenos Aires and the great mines collapsed, so did the vast trade in mules and provisions to the mines, the lifeblood of these provinces. Recently, times have been tough.

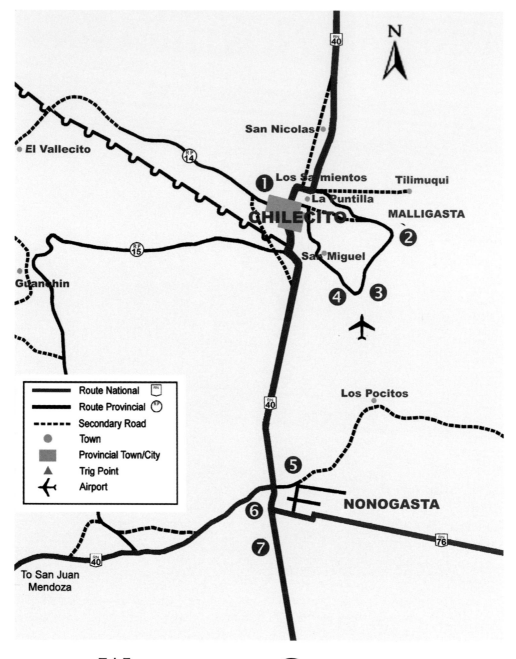

WINERIES OF CHILECITO

Position: 29.18S 67.42W

	Bodega	Address	Town	
1	La Riojana Cooperative	Publica s/n	Chilecito	5360
2	Motegay	Fraccion 7	Chileceto	5360
3	Soc. Nacari	Joaquin s/n	Chilecito	5360
4	Aguinan	Aguinan s/n	Chilecito	5360

LA RIOJA PROVINCE

From San Juan, it is 515 kilometres further north to La Rioja, founded in 1591 as Todos los Santos de las Nueva Rioja. Here one enters the Andean North West, where the great cordillera starts to broaden out. The nearly 9,000 km long Andes mountain range is relatively young and still subject to violent earthquakes and eruptions. All Argentine wine cities have been destroyed at some time or another. La Rioja had its last destructive earthquake in 1894.

Having reached the capital, there is still another long, slow 190 km travel to reach the wine region of Chilecito, not to be confused with Chilecito in Mendoza's Uco Valley. The main producer, one of South America's largest and certainly most competent and energetic cooperatives, La Riojana, is located in Chilecito. This town was originally known as Santa Rita but mining the gold of Famatina attracted so many Chileans that the town was renamed.

Home to poets and the current president, Chilecito is also home to 33,000 people and the center of an impressive tourist industry which includes Nonogasta, Cuesta de Miranda and Villa Unión. The region is locally described as the land of *red, green* and *blue.* These are the colors that typify the spectacular red of the canyon walls, the lush green of the vineyards and fields — and the blue, blue sky. As an example of knockout scenery, the unpaved 56 km road from Chilecito to Cuesta de Miranda has 800 turns!

In winter, devoid of its green vineyards, Chilecito is a modern day version of a Hollywood western movie town; dry, barren and isolated. But don't be fooled by appearances, the town has a university campus, a regular air service and all the amenities of life in the 21st century; even a restaurant named Chaplin. Local food is excellent, accommodation sparse and rather ordinary.

Despite its isolation, more than a 1,000 winelovers from all over the world visit the local wineries each week during the holiday seasons.

Wine is grown in 11 departments of La Rioja though centralization of the cooperative industry restricts production to four departments; there are 38 bodegas in all. Bounded by the Velasco Mountains in the east and Famatina Ranges in the west, the grape varieties reflect La Rioja's hot, arid climate. Torrontes Riojana represents 55 percent of all plantings and Cabernet only five percent. Other red varieties are Barbera (15 percent), Merlot (10 percent) and Malbec (5 percent).

This is the home province of Carlos Saul Menem, a former provincial governor, who changed from being a Muslim to Roman Catholic so that he could become the nation's president. It is also the home of Juan Perón's third wife, Isabelita.

121

A colorful storage tank at La Riojana Cooperative.

Author's Choice

Torrontés Riojana

LA RIOJANA COOPERATIVE

When one talks about wine in La Rioja province, this means the *cooperativa*. Founded in 1940, this dynamic local concern today has nearly 640 grower-members. La Riojana Cooperative is big and their wines are distributed nationally and overseas.

One can only comprehend its size by understanding that there are a total of seven winery locations, five owned by the cooperative and two others leased. La Riojana has two sites in Chilecito, one each in the towns of Nonogasta, Villa Union and Banda Florida. The combined storage capacity of these seven wineries is a staggering 49 million litres.

The cooperative has a varying range of wines starting with 4.7 litre demi-johns. Next is a range of one litre Tetra packs named El Montonero and Vinas Riojanas.

In cork-finished 750 ml bottles, the range commences with the Vinas Riojanas label which, unbelievably, sells for well under US$2 per bottle in the domestic market. Top of the range is the export label Santa Florentina which features a flowery Torrontes, red Barbera, Cabernet Sauvignon and an excellent Malbec.

There are new plantings of Syrah and Cabernet in selected areas — and the cooperative is undergoing trials with oak ageing of red wines. This forward looking company has also developed their own fermentation yeasts selected from vineyards within the province.

In addition to using their members' own grapes, the cooperative buys from non-member growers and also purchases wine from other La Rioja producers for their expanding international markets.

These include the principal markets such as the U.K., North America, and newer markets in Scandinavia and Estonia. South American countries have long been traditional importers.

A really exciting product is Torrontes "champagne", a sparkling wine with intense fruit flavor. Other products from the cooperative are grape juice, mineral water, olives in brine, nuts and raisins.

The people of Chilecito are very special people in a very special place. One can only stand in awe of what they have achieved in so many fields in this remote desert oasis; wine quality in particular.

At a recent Argentine wine event in San Francisco, California, featuring many of the country's better wines, one respected wine columnist said that the best of the 100 or so wines on display was the La Florentina Torrontes.

La Rioja - a land of stunning contrasts.

DESERT INNOVATION

Yeast is the heart and soul of the magic of fermentation which provides us with such wonderful foods as bread, cheese, beer, whisky and wine. Winemakers become attached to their favorite yeasts, which convert sugar to alcohol, and at times become either romantic or irrational about the use of this product in the creation of their artistry.

Experts in the field of yeast production will tell you that the job of yeast is to complete the fermentation, then get out of the way without leaving any undesirable after-effects which can be numerous. As the flavor of the finished wine is almost "set-in-stone" during the primary fermentation, the choice of the correct yeast is paramount.

La Riojana Cooperative were so concerned about the sameness of their white wines using imported yeasts that they made a courageous decision to do something original; develop their own yeast strain from local vineyards. To work in wine, yeasts require very specific conditions in relation to temperature and alcohol tolerance. Under ideal conditions the correct yeast will give a good alcohol yield from the sugar available, provide good esters and higher alcohols - and work at a desirable speed without foaming.

The La Riojana people who tackled this task were a group of ordinary winemakers and quality control technicians in an isolated oasis, in the high desert country of western Argentina. In the 1980s they had no access to sophisticated city labs just around the corner.

After considerable vineyard research, the breakthrough came in 1994 when they isolated four strains that prevailed in the fermentation of the grape variety Torrontes Riojano. Eventually one strain was selected and named LRV-945. The program was then taken national - tested at the INTA research station and by wineries in Salta, San Juan and Mendoza.

Following these tests it was franchised by a major French yeast laboratory who asked 16 Argentine wineries to test and compare it with the wineries own favored yeast. The upshot of these experiments saw 15 of the 16 participants favoring the LRV 945 over the yeasts currently in use at their own bodegas. This was a major commercial breakthrough.

A fairy tale ending - the flower of the desert is now commercially available in dry yeast form and, to this time, the cooperative have not had to buy any of their own yeast.

125

AWESOME ARGENTINA

Desert sunrise near Cafayate - above. The Cafayate canyons - below.

Salta Province

Tobacco, bananas and sugar cane are also grown in the tropical Andean north which indicates the diversity of climate. Salta province, with but 15 bodegas, has two wineries with international distribution. At 1,900 metres, Salta's Cafayate region has Argentina's, and one of the world's, highest vineyards. The main vineyards are at an elevation of 1,400 to 1,600 metres.

Most wine regions of the world are attractive tourist destinations but nowhere in the world is there a more awesome, in every sense of the word, destination than Salta, considered Argentina's best preserved colonial town. The city is named for an Indian word *sagta* meaning "the very beautiful one".

Salta also offers *peñas folklóricas* eating houses where you enjoy food, wine, guitar music and traditional dancing. The reservoirs in the cordillera provide for water enthusiasts and the many streams offer good fishing. The Andes has an abundance of national parks in all provinces for trekking. Salta has a particularly good park, Parque Nacional Los Cardones, home to a unique candelabra cactus commonly used for building.

The wine regions of Salta are nearly 200 km or three hours south of the capital, in fact, very close to the Catamarca provincial boundary.

The drive from the capital to the wine regions is one of unimaginable splendor, through the ever-changing canyons (*quebrada*) of the Conchas River, better known as the Quebrada de Cafayate. This is a place for very careful driving; it is a long fall from the mountainside road to the river! In only a few hours travel from Salta the visitor will see verdant fields, the unbelievable canyons of multi-colored sandstone, and, approaching Cafayate, an area of vast sand dunes.

Unlike the provinces to the south, parts of Salta enjoy plentiful rainfall. There are heavy downpours in the cordillera that have, over the centuries, created extraordinary canyons with thought-provoking names such as *Los Castillos* (The Castles), *Garganta del Diablo* (Devil's Throat) and *El Anfiteatro* (The Amphitheatre).

Cafayate is a wine town, complete with a museum and excellent visitor facilities at several wineries. This quaint little town offers plain accommodations, yet superior parilladas and empanadas for those who enjoy local food. Further to the north and west of Cafayate, in the stunning Calchaquies Valley, the vine also flourishes around San Carlos and Molinos, towns more than 2000 km from Buenos Aires.

Cafayate wines, built around Torrontes, Chardonnay, Malbec and Cabernet, are recognized around the world as being marvelous value-for-money wines.

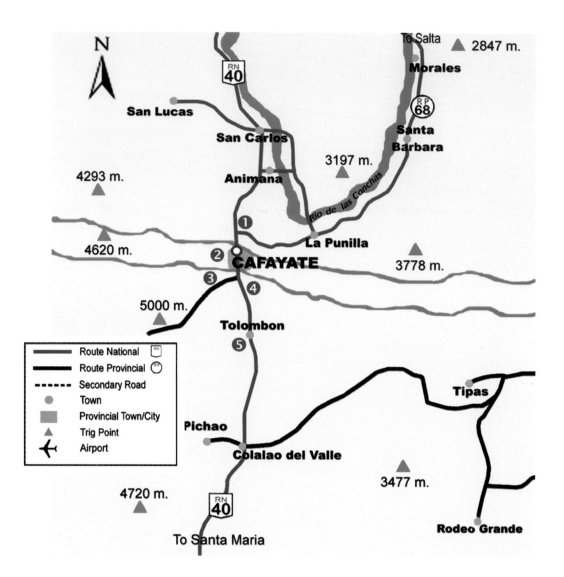

WINERIES OF CAFAYATE REGION

Position: 24.50S 65.16W

Bodega	Address	Town	
1. Michel Torino	Finca La Rosa	Cafayate	4427
2. Domingo Hnos	25 Mayo s/n	Cafayate	4427
3. El Recreo	Calle Vecinal s/n	Cafayate	4427
4. Arnaldo Etchart	Finca La Florida	Cafayate	4427
5. Cavas de Santa Maria	RN 40	Cafayate	4427

WINE ASSOCIATIONS

Argentina has a number of associations to serve all facets of wine growing, production, research, marketing, inspection and policing. Sadly for people interested in Argentine wine, most are ineffective and uncooperative when it comes to seeking information.

The most effective and useful body would be the Centro de Bodegueros de Mendoza, or, the Wine Center of Mendoza. It is a pity that they have such a disconcerting name as they do not have facilities to service any public needs. This is a century old association of producers who banded together in the bad old days when Mendoza was on a different planet to Buenos Aires. Over the years they have served their members well in many ways. They are responsible for Mendoza's showpiece, the annual Wine Festival.

Centro de Bodegueros de Mendoza - Rivadavia 592, 5500 Mendoza

Fax: 54 61 244 477

Instituto Nacional Vitiviniculture (INV) is a government body empowered to control all aspects of the growing and production sides of the industry; it loosely helps in marketing. INV is also the link with international associations. In addition to drawing-up all sorts of rules and regulations, the Institute maintains a large laboratory for quality control of export wine. INV also maintains industry statistics but any appeal to this bureaucratic body for help is akin to mounting a Mt. Everest expedition.

Instituto Nacional Vitiviniculture - San Martin 430, 5500 Mendoza

Fax: 54 61 343 3846

The very name Argentine Vitivinicultural Association (AVA) suggests that here is one body that might assist those in need of information. Not so; not only do they not assist, they are aggressively rude about their lack of desire to help. AVA is a collection of about 28 exporters whose sole aim is the promotion of their members' products in the export market. Fair enough, but could they not refer enquirers to the appropriate people - a service that most people in business do every day?

Asociacion Vitivincola Argentina - Guemes 4464, (1425) Buenos Aires

Fax: 54 1 776 2529

129

MICHEL TORINO

BODEGA LA ROSA

VINO FINO TINTO

Elaborado y envasado por Bodega Michel Torino Hnos. S.A.I.C.A. - INV N° S-73121
En Ruta 68 - Cafayate - Salta - Valles Calchaquíes - Industria Argentina - Cont. Neto **750cm³**

Author's Choice

Don David Cabernet

Finca La Rosa, Cafayate, Salta province

MICHEL TORINO

One of the best known labels of long-standing in Argentina is Michel Torino from Cafayate. Its solid reputation has been built on quality wines at favorable prices. That alone is quite an achievement when one considers that its wines are made just short of 2,000 km from the major market. The siblings of the Michel and Torino families married and the combination made a national enterprise from their prime La Rosa estate which comprises two of the country's most arresting neo-Spanish homesteads.

In a way, it is a pity that the forbears did not live to see the current results of their initial labors. Nowhere in the world is there such a modern day winery catering with such splendor for royalty, heads-of-state and the public-at-large. Winelovers from around the globe come here in large numbers. Everything in the way of tourist facilities, including a top restaurant, are available to all and sundry but the very upscale accommodation is reserved for VIPs. The surgery at the La Rosa estate was so drastic that even the local school was flattened to make way for landscaping the grand entrance. An improved school has been built on a better site.

Not that far from the Bolivian and Chilean borders, the wineries of Cafayate, Michel Torino in particular, have become trendsetters in winery hospitality in South America. Yet this is only the show-front of the operation; even more exciting things are happening in the vineyards and winery.

Fully cognizant that good wine is made in the vineyard, Michel Torino engaged renowned Australian viticulturist, Dr. Richard Smart, to consult with resident vineyard chief, Andres Hoy. Together they have modified the traditional Argentine parral trellising to produce vastly improved fruit which obviously reflects in the wine quality.

Even though the corporation is fully committed in Cafayate they are involved in further major expansion of 400 ha at Santa Maria, 75 km south in nearby Catamarca province. Here the soil is stony and similar to France's southern Rhone region where the Syrah vine grows so well. This is in direct contrast to the almost powdery soil of the home blocks at La Rosa which are lacking in nitrogen and organic matter.

Located at nearly 2,000 metres, the Santa Maria vineyard is the highest fine table wine vineyard in the world. However, there are higher vineyards in India and Mexico for sparkling wines. Cabernet, Merlot and Malbec are the principal varieties but, contrary to good advice, a substantial area has surprisingly been planted to Pinot noir; this should be watched with special interest.

131

Author's Choice
Privada Torrontés

ETCHART

On a comfortable walk south of Cafayate township along the Route National 40, the visitor will cross the River Colorado (sans water!), pass the El Recero vineyards of Michel Torino and arrive at the well-appointed tourist facility of Etchart on the left of the road. The winery and offices are opposite.

The winery, vineyards and mountain backdrop are an impressive sight. As the region boasts 350 sunny days annually, much of the extensive winery is outdoors; still, the openness of the indoor winery has superb views of these impressive mountains.

This is a unique grape growing region and Finca La Florida is a unique and old vineyard with one criolla vine dating back to 1862! Today there are 300 ha of vineyards with the big emphasis on Torrontés and Malbec.

However, in a world that still wants to drink Cabernet regardless of whether it comes from Bolivia or Bulgaria, Cabernet is a popular variety in Cafayate. There is a varietal Cafayate Cabernet and an Arnaldo B blend, dominated by Cabernet, which is made in new oak.

Due to its elevation of nearly 1,700 metres above sea level, the whites of Cafayate, fortunately, have a distinctive style and while Torrontés is the superstar, Chenin is proving to be an ideal variety for this region. Chardonnay is doing well also. It is fair to say here that Torrontés is an overwhelmingly powerful wine in terms of aroma and flavor, and the average English-speaking consumer would consider one glass sufficient. Much the same can be said for most other aromatic varieties such as the Muscats and Gewurztraminer — and, to a lesser extent, Sauvignon (blanc). Etchart have both a Privada and a Cafayate Torrontés label.

While Torrontés is the Argentine signature white wine, it would not be wise to predicate a future on enormous sales of this wine unless fairly wisely blended with a more neutral variety such as Chenin. One can feel sure that their Orlando colleague, distinguished South Australian winemaker Robin Day, will steer them on a correct commercial course.

In summary, the Etchart Cafayate wines are a very sound commercial range of value-for-money wines and the winelover can look forward to some surprises in the future.

133

Women in Wine

During an Argentine wine dinner in San Francisco, California, the main topic of conversation became womens place in Argentine business. These successful women all agreed that things have changed rather favorably for them in recent times.

If one was to make a study of the marketing side of the wine business it would appear that the export business would not happen if it was not for women. While a lot of Argentine men might like to think that they are the operators or decision makers, there is absolutely no doubt that women are doing their fair share of the effective work; in companies large and small.

Three of the major players - Catena group, La Agricola and Trapiche - have decided that women do it best in export markets. The men become very visible when there are all-expenses paid trips to England, France, USA etc., the very same people are invisible in the day-to-day operations at home; women are doing the work!

Catena's Marina Gayán, a charming and talented young lady, is responsible for marketing Argentina's finest wines. With her team at Catena/Esmeralda, La Rural and Escorihuela, Marina designs sophisticated packaging, labels and marketing strategies. She then appears at very selected trade shows around world extremely proud of her efforts.

La Agricola's Cecilia Fernandez, mother of two young men, has a similar, but different role. She does the same things as Marina, but the Santa Julia and other La Agricola labels are at the other end of the market. They are canvassed far more aggressively and to wider markets.

Mother and daughter combination, Alicia and Dolores Lavaque, certainly represent the finest in Argentine tailoring. Immaculately groomed when presenting their Lavaque and Michel Torino wines, they always look as though they've just stepped out of a boutique. Dolores is the full-time export director; mother comes along to lend a hand.

While being definitely a minor force in the bodega at this time, women are taking a larger role in the vineyards. Maybe much of this has to do with the broader Spanish education of agronomists which graduates students to cover both fruit and viticulture; the English graduate is more specialized in viticulture alone. Two of the countries larger firms, Bianchi in San Rafael and the Cooperative in La Rioja, entrust their vineyards to the tender care of women.

With much experience, Susana Balbo is the only woman who heads a winery but she does have a number of colleagues

WOMEN IN WINE

who are playing their part in winemaking teams. Susana worked for some in Salta where she specialized in taming the powerful Torrontés aroma and its other bad habits such as oxidation. She speaks with considerable passion about this grape.

Adriana Elena Martinez has been an assistant to the brilliant Walter Brescia at Nieto and Senetiner since 1989. Adriana has traveled widely in Europe sharpening her winemaking skills in all facets of table and sparkling winemaking.

Flichman have recently added Silvia Corti to their technical team. Silvia has a varied background that expounds the diversity of Mendoza. Included in her experience is work in mass production of tomatoes and the production of radishes, lettuces, cabbages & garlic - strange bedfellows for a winemaker!

Winemakers three - Silvia Avignina, Adriana Martinez & Susana Balbo

Marketers three - Cecila Fernandez above - Mom & daughter Alicia & Dolores Lavaque.

Catena group marketing guru - Marina Gayán

Dr. Nicolas Catena, quiet powerhouse of Argentine wine

136

THE CONSCIENCE OF ARGENTINA WINE

When domestic wine was easy to sell in Argentina at $1 per litre and profits were astronomical, one man realized that this was not the future for either his company — or Argentina. The value of quality was forcibly driven home to Nicolas Catena following a visit to California's most modern winery in 1976. Being familiar with numerous European wines, Nicolas was struck by what was happening in California and the power of the fruit in the wines; this was really different.

In 1982 this man of many hats was a visiting agricultural economics professor at the University of California (UC), Berkeley. Every spare moment during this stay was utilized visiting California's north coast wineries, listening, and observing what was happening in this hothouse of experimentation. It was this experience that was the turning point for Esmeralda - and, probably South America.

He learned that Argentina was doing it all wrong and things must be different, in the vineyards, and the winery. This is the conscience part of this man. He has invested heavily in research with the mission of discovering the ideal conditions for the cultivation of correct varieties, in the right places. In this he has succeeded.

During the 20 plus years since his momentous California visit, Dr. Catena has climbed every peak of wine stardom, even though wine represents only 20 percent of his business interests. These include salt production, mining and household fittings.

Yet, he is a wine producer and industrialist by default. At heart he is a scholar; he always wanted a scholar's life, not a winemaker. His father Domingo, and grandfather, Nicolas, were winemakers — his mother a scholar. Family tradition is very strong in this culture; Nicolas, a good student, became a winery executive.

His application for entry to the University of Chicago as a doctoral student in economics was accepted in 1963. This brought about his life's greatest dilemma — school or family, a decision resolved in favor of winegrowing. Nicolas Catena did eventually complete his doctoral dissertation at Columbia University, New York, in 1973.

The family wine business was started in 1902 by his Italian emigrant grandfather. At the time of young Nicolas' graduation in 1973 the business was suffering a financial crisis, a situation in which a trained economist could help. He soon realized that he belonged in this business world and in a few months took over the role of chief executive.

For this modest man, wine became a passion, yet this high achiever knows he can always do better. His enthusiasm and drive make him an object lesson for all South American winemakers. Why? Because he has consistently been a leader of new winery and vineyard technology introducing the latest Australian and European technology

137

USEFUL ADDRESSES

ALLIED DOMECQ BALBI
L.N Alem Avenue 1110 10th floor
1001 BUENOS AIRES
Fax: 54 1 3134462

NAVARRO CORREAS
Don Bosco 3672, 2°
1206 BUENOS AIRES
Fax: 54 1 9592878

BODEGA NORTON S.A.
Trelles 2669
1416 BUENOS AIRES
Fax: 54 61 880 482

BODEGAS ETCHART S.A.
Lima 229 - 3° Piso
1073 BUENOS AIRES
Fax: 54 3826923/3820310

BODEGAS ESMERALDA S.A.
Guatemala 4565
1425 BUENOS AIRES
Fax: 54 1 832 3086

BIANCHI VALENTIN
Comandante Torres 500
5600 SAN RAFAEL (MENDOZA)
Fax: 54 62730131

BODEGAS TRAPICHE S.A.
Nueva Mayorga S/N, Coquimbito
5513 MAIPU (MENDOZA)
Fax: 54 61 973737

BODEGAS Y VINEDOS SANTA ANA S.A.
Reconquista 538, Piso
1003 BUENOS AIRES
Fax: 54 1 3932388

CASA VINICOLA NIETO Y SENETINER
Chile 955
5500 MENDOZA
Fax: 54 61 236558

FINCA FLICHMAN S.A.
av. Corrientes 1891 - Piso 4°
1045 BUENOS AIRES
Fax: 54 1 3753449/13720579

JOSE BORBORE S.A.C.I.A.F.
Colon S/N San Martin
5439 SAN JUAN
Fax: 54 64 971040

LA AGRICOLA S.A.
Chuquisaca 200
5547 GODOY CRUZ (MENDOZA)
Fax: 54 61 272468

LA RIOJANA, LTDA COOPERATIVA
La Plata, 646
5360 CHILECITO (LA RIOJA)
Fax: 54 82523299

LAGARDE, S.A.
San Martin, 1745
5507 LUJAN DE CUYO (MENDOZA)
Fax: 54 61 981392

LEONCIO ARIZU SA
San Martin 2044
5507 LUJAN DE CUYO (MENDOZA)
Fax: 54 1 8314658

MICHEL TORINO HERMANOS S.A.I.C.A.
Godoy Cruz 3236 - 2° Piso
1425 BUENOS AIRES
Fax: 54 7759733

S.A. BODEGAS CHANDON
Florida 378 Pisos 5 y 6
1351 BUENOS AIRES
Fax: 54 1 12927

BODEGAS GRAFFIGNA LTDA.
Cuenca 560
1672 VILLA LYNCH   SAN MARTIN Bs As
Fax: 54 1 7542593

S.A.I.A. PASCUAL TOSO
Alberdi 808
5519 SAN JOSE (MENDOZA)
Fax: 54 61 456678

WHEN THE SAINTS COME MARCHING IN!

A buyer stands looking at the wine shelves wanting to replace last night's favorite bottle but can't remember which of the saints was enjoyed by all.

Was it Santa Maria, Santa Rita or Santos Ricardo (all the saints) or did it come from the saint of Carrodilla or Lujan? To those unsaintly ones of British stock, sorting out the saints of South American wine is about as confusing as an Argentine trying to understand what's happening at a cricket match - particularly when the game stops for tea and lunch!

Saint George was a real big hero in the British world, so much so that they included his cross on the flag. He has a grape named for him in Greece, a vineyard in New Zealand, also a wine in Australia, but other than that his fame has been restricted to the parish church.

As far as saints go in the New World, Saint Clement gets the odd mention and Australia has weighed in with an All Saints winery but, generally, saints are left to their own clerical world; wine is wine and church is religion.

Not so for the Latins who love a real fruit salad of saints and wine.

Argentina's contribution is fairly weighty with an even mix of males and females; Santa Ana, Santa Florentina, Santa Isabel and Santa Julia while the fellows are San Carlos, San Felipe, Saint Sylvie, Saint Remy, Saint Valerie and Saint Felicien to name a few.

Of course, these saintly wines could come from a choice of San Luis, San Jose, San Juan, San Martin, San Rafael or San Telmo. The ultimate saintly wine must be St.Remy, Avenue San Martin 363, San Juan.

This maybe OK for some, yet the real job of a wine label is to be an advertisement and informative. A label should also be an invitation, an indication of status and a visiting card that invites one to share its contents. It should attract and provide a visual foretaste of what lies within, and, finally, it should not confuse the buyer. More so when Argentine wines are usually on the shelves next to Chilean wines which also have their share of saintly brews.

Now that the Californians have come-up with a Santa Evita wine, let us hope another enterprising soul will introduce a Diego Maradona wine - now there's a real saint!

ARGENTINE TRAVEL

There are several ways to reach Argentina on either direct flights to Buenos Aires Ezeiza (EZE) international airport or through many of the other South American countries. The national carrier *Aerolinas Argentinas* does not receive a very high rating and is probably the most expensive South American carrier. However, it does provide a direct link from most continents but very poor from the U.K. Alternatives are with the Brazilian carrier *Varig* through San Paulo, *Aero Peru* via Lima, *Lloyd Aero Boliviano* via La Paz and *Lan Chile* via Mexico City and Santiago. *Lan Chile* is a so-so airline and winter flights through Santiago are regularly half to one day late.

Should you be traveling to Mendoza in winter, you can have the ridiculous scenario of being diverted from Santiago to Mendoza, unable to leave the aircraft for many hours (without food, drink or information), fly back to Santiago when the weather has cleared and then catch a connecting flight back to Mendoza. Lost luggage is a major problem with *Lan Chile*. The writer's own experience suggests that they do not compensate in anyway for their inefficiency.

Lufthansa, Air France, American, British, United and other major carriers all give good service to both Santiago and Buenos Aires EZE. However, if going onto Mendoza or other domestic airports, it is necessary to travel right across Buenos Aires city to the downtown Aeroparque (AEP) domestic terminal. It is this incovenient connection that makes the Santiago-Mendoza a desirable option — and you do get to fly over the Andes!

Most South American pilots are "sporty" by comparison with English-language carriers — doing many low, tight turns on approach which may be something new, even for seasoned travelers.

By any standards, Argentine airports are grossly inefficient, due mainly to the national airport police force which runs at about 40 percent effectiveness. Be prepared for long queues and irregular departure and arrival times.

After the giant Brazil, Argentina is the largest country on the South American continent. The minimum distance from the capital, Buenos Aires, to the wine country is 1,000 km east to west. The distance from the highly recommended northern wine areas to the southern region of General Roca is 1,800 km, north to south.

Rental cars

The vast distances, incredibly expensive rental cars, high gasoline costs, rather ordinary roads and persistent police check points don't make for pleasant driving. As in Chile and Peru, the police have compulsory check points, at least every 100 km, on almost every road, just in case motorists get lost on the only highway — or for some other needless and bureaucratic reason. This unwelcome police intrusion would be unacceptable in most other countries and unconstituitional in the USA.

140

Road Transportation

One facet of the Argentine, in fact South American, tourism/hospitality industries, that works with amazing efficiency is the intra and inter country long distance bus (coach) services. Nearly every city has a central bus station that will take the traveler anywhere on the continent, regularly and effectively. Even on a two hour trip covering a meal time, passengers will mostly be treated to a light luncheon included in the modest price of the ticket. These coaches are modern, well-equipped and run to schedule; recommended.

Taxis

Throughout Argentina there are two options: regular black and yellow cabs and a service called *remise* which cannot be hailed on the street. The remise service, which is highly recommended, will cost slightly more but is worth every every extra cent in terms of safety, direct (via the shortest route) to your destination, cleanliness and courtesy.

Domestic airlines

The frightening alternative is the domestic airline service. *Aerolinas Argentinas* and their subsidiary, *Austral,* run the most expensive services to almost every wine centre from Bs.As. Aeroparque. Full-jet discount carriers *Lapa, Dinair, Southern Winds* and others offer equally good services at considerably reduced prices. However, to make the say, 300 km trip from one wine centre to the next, requires a 2,000 km round trip via Aeroparque. Mendoza-based Andesmar prop-jets offer north-south, milk-run flights to wine centres along the Andes at reasonable prices. The flight from Mendoza to Salta has four stops, but positively beats driving.

Communications

The now privatized telephone companies have lifted their game considerably, but nowhere near the competency of neighboring Chile. Costs are almost prohibitive in so much as many business calls within Argentina are routed by cheaper carriers in Miami, USA! Due to these costs, most small businesses have joint telephone/fax lines which means that it is nearly always necessary to call your party and advise that a fax is coming. The mail service is normal?

Dining

Argentine restaurants, once very cheap, have learned that the world is awash in money and in recent years prices have skyrocketed. Nonetheless, they offer excellent food of many cuisines with professional service and without fuss; wine prices are very reasonable by any standard. As can be expected, Italian restaurants dominate the food scene but it is easy to find a favorable alternative. Argentine food, be it meat or vegetables, is as good as can be obtained anywhere in the world, and the combination fresh salads are the very best. Naturally, larger city restaurants run the gamut of extremely expensive to modest prices. So long as late hours don't bother the traveler, restaurants do not open before 9pm — eating out in Argentina is a rewarding and pleasant experience.

People

Nowhere in the world will the traveler find more friendly, hospitable and helpful people. Understanding that their culture varies enormously from that of most English-speaking cultures, the people are Argentina's greatest tourist asset.

ARGENTINE CHEESE

Wine and cheese, two of our most wonderful natural foods are both products of the magic of fermentation. Give 10 wine or cheese makers the same raw materials for their craft and they will each produce a different product; such is the hand of humans - men or women. In the case of cheese it can be made from the milk of camels, goats, sheep, yaks, llamas or cows and the quality and style of the resultant cheese will depend mainly on the land on which the animals graze. Hot arid conditions or lush green pastures will produce very different fare.

Like wine, cheese has been with us for thousands of years - archeologists show evidence of 4000BC - and has much the same historical background. Born in Egypt, then to Greece, it was the Romans who introduced cheese through Europe as we know it today. Ghengis Khan took it to Asia and the Crusaders returned with exotic spices to further enhance their home products.

Cheese has played an interesting part in history. David was actually delivering cheese to Saul when he met the giant, but history does not record whether he ate some fortifying cheese before his battle with Goliath.

It is said that the final straw in the Bounty mutiny resulted from an argument between Fletcher Christian and Capt. Bligh over cheese. Yet a more interesting South American dispute was resolved when the American-led Uruguayan navy achieved victory over the British-led Argentine navy by finally firing Dutch Edam cheese balls when they ran out of the more conventional cannon balls. Do I smell a rat?

The origin of the word cheese is an interesting lesson in linguistics. *Formos* was the name given to Greek cheese made in a basket, the Romans translated this to *formage* the Italians to *formaggio*, the French to *fromage*. From the Latin came the word *caseus* while the Germans used *kasse*, the Dutch *kaas*, and somewhere along the line in Spanish it became *queso*. Across the Channel the Irish used *cais*, the Welsh word is *caws* and the English originally knew it as *caise* and *cease* which evolved as *ches*, *chiese*, *schese* and finally cheese.

Argentine cheese may sound something of an oxymoron to European purists but to a country with vast cattle herds and a strong European background, cheese is as natural south of the Equator as it is in the north. In fact, most of the Southern Hemisphere countries such as Argentina, Chile, New Zealand and Australia have vibrant cheese industries.

The cheeselands of Argentina stretch 3000 km from the far north almost to Cape Horn. Many areas produce only cow's milk cheese. The Rio Gallegos region, which looks at the Falklands Islands from near the Straits of Magellan, is renowned for its cheese made from sheep's milk. The artisan produced goat's milk cheese is a coming product. Well established in the northern provinces of Salta and Jujuy, there is an important production center in southern San Luis province.

ARGENTINE CUISINE

An Introduction By
Dereck Foster

Argentine cuisine — true, native cooking — does not exist. Argentina and its inhabitants enjoy an inherited cuisine, incorporating first the traditions of Spain, then Italy, and later a medley of basically European influences including a strong seasoning of Middle-Eastern traditions. Much of the Arab influence originally arrived somewhat modified via Spain (which had undergone four centuries of Arab domination) to be reinforced later by a strong influx of immigrants from Syria, Lebanon and Mediterranean environs.

The Americas have offered many treasures to the world, such as the potato, the tomato, corn (maize), chocolate (cocoa), peppers and so much more, overlooked Argentina in this distribution. Argentina with its fertile pampas, vast windswept plains of Patagonia, the wooded and forested North, and semi-arid Andean foothills and plains had nothing to offer the first white settlers. Potatoes came mainly from the Andean highlands of Peru, maize from further north as well as all the rest of the American bounty.

Argentina had to adopt its basic ingredients from abroad, including the wheat, beef and mutton which formed (and still partially forms) the basis of its wealth. Even the typically "native" dishes one comes across, mostly away from the city of Buenos Aires which tries to shun its colonial past, are becoming harder to find as time passes.

The recipes given in the following selection of Argentine dishes are fairly representative but not as widespread as one might believe. They try to reflect, however, the general trend of Argentine eating habits. The lack of fowl, fish and mutton (or lamb) in the selection is as much due to local tastes as to shortage of space in this book.

143

The basic ingredients of empanadas criolla

Two styles of emapanadas criolla

144

The Starters

Empanadas

Serves: 4   *Time*: 40 minutes

Empanadas are a popular snack and starter throughout the Spanish speaking countries of South America. They are a turnover in the Cornish pastie mold. There are innumerable variations in Argentina of both the fillings - and the cooking method. Empanadas can be fried or baked. This is a popular baked recipe.

Pastry: **1.5 kg flour - 400 g lard - 1 1/2 cups warm water - 1 tsp salt**

Method: Make a hole in centre of flour, pour in warm melted lard, then water in which salt has been dissolved. Work dough until smooth without lumps, (approx. 15 min). Cover and rest 20 min. Roll out pastry to about ½ cm thick, with a large cup or mold, cut disks.

Filling: **250g lard, ½ kg ground beef - 1 kg spring onions, chopped - 1 tbs chopped parsley - pinch cumin - pinch dry oregano - I tbs hot paprika - 5 hard-boiled eggs, sliced - 200 gr seedless raisins - 500 g green olives.**

Method: Lightly fry onions. Add paprika and beef which has been parboiled 30 seconds. Mix in rest , save the eggs, raisins and olives. Cook 3-4 minutes; let cool. Place some of this fry in centre of the discs, add an olive, a few raisins, a slice of egg, fold pastry over. Wet pastry edges with water, press with a fork to seal well. Prick top of each empanada several times with a toothpick. Bake in hot oven 4 min. or until slightly browned.

Wine: Argentines have a strong preference for red (tinto) wines. A lighter style Malbec is ideal with empanadas.

Albondigas de Pollo

(Chicken balls)

Serves: 4   *Time*: 40 minutes

Although beef is the staple meat diet, chicken runs a good second. This is a favorite chicken starter, ideal for a patio party.

Ingredients: **2 chicken breasts - 5 tbs breadcumbs - 1 egg - 1 cup broth - 1 tbs butter**

Method: Finely chop or mince breasts. Mix into beaten egg and breadcrumbs. Season with salt to taste. Boil the broth with butter, make balls or croquettes with the chicken mixture and boil a few at a time for 10-12 minutes. Can be eaten hot or cold.

Wine: Torrontés is always a fun starter

The Entrees

Centolla (King Crab) Salad

Serves: 4   *Time*: 20 minutes

Centolla is the King crab from Tierra del Fuego and is the island's top product. The waters of the Beagle Channel are shared by Argentina and Chile and are rich with crab. Both countries claim the crab as their own!

Ingredients: **1kg cooked centolla (King crab) meat - 2 tbs cream - 2 tbs butter - 3 avocado pears peeled and cut in strips - 1 egg- 1 lemon - pinch Cayenne pepper - salt and black pepper.**

Method: Arrange avocado slices on large serving dish, place roughly chopped crab meat on top. Partly melt butter, beat in cream and egg to obtain a thickish cream. Add lemon juice, Cayenne pepper; season with salt and black pepper to taste. Pour cream over crab, garnish with parsley - serve chilled.

Wine: Is there anything better than sparkling wine (champagne) with crab?

Corn and Sausage Scramble

Serves: 4   *Time*: 25 minutes

This is the food of the Pampas gaucho. Easily and quickly prepared, it is very nourishing and simple fare.

Ingredients: **2 cups corn kernels, cooked - 200 g pork sausage, cut in 1 cm. lengths - 1 small chopped onion - 4 beaten eggs - oil, salt and pepper.**

Method: In a heavy skillet, lightly fry onions in as little oil as possible (sausage will add its own). When ready, fry sausage pieces until well done. Stir in the corn and mix well. Pour in beaten eggs, condiment with salt and pepper and stir until eggs are firm.

Serve hot. (The elegant way is to pile the scramble on pieces of fried bread).

Wine: Chenin (blanc)

146

Main Course

Parillada

Serves: Many   *Time:* 40 minutes

Grilled and roasted meats are an important part of the Argentine diet. The typical asado (barbeque) can be a simple or a massive affair, including many cuts of beef which are unknown in Europe or the US, as well as variety meats and offal, such as udder and chitterlings.

An asado which includes anything thrown onto a grill is called a parillada. An asado which uses a spit is not technically a parillada but an asado al spiedo or al asador.

In a typical parillada one will normally find at least one type of sausage, blood sausage (morcilla), sweetbreads, chitterlings, rib roast cut in strips (tira de asado) and some other cut which could be tenderloin, vaccio (a local cut off the underbelly) or matambre (also a local cut from the underbelly), even some goat.

Chicken is usually grilled on its own. Pork and lamb, almost without exception, are cooked on a spit set in the ground and leaning slightly over the open fire.

This type of meal is served with a green salad which includes tomato and onion, and chimichurri, a spicy hot sauce made with herbs, oil and vinegar.

Carbonada

Serves: 4   *Time:* 40 minutes

Carbonada is a typical stew from the north-west. There are several versions of this delicious winter stew. This is a popular recipe that is easy to prepare.

Ingredients: **750 g stewing beef - 6 tbs chicken fat (or lard) - 2 cups rice - 1 kg pumpkin - 1 large onion - 3 peeled, seedless tomatoes - 1 sweet pepper - 2 large corn cobs cut into 3-4 pieces each - 1 teaspoon sweet paprika - 1 tablespoon sugar - 2 peeled cubed potatoes - 2 litres beef broth - salt and pepper to taste.**

Method: Lightly fry chopped onion and pepper in the fat until starting to brown. Add chopped tomatoes, the paprika and a little salt. Partly brown the beef in some fat - and also the rice partly in more fat. When lightly browned, drain and add to previous mixture. Pour in the broth and potatoes. Simmer 15 minutes then add chopped pumpkin pieces. Cook 10 minutes more then add the corn pieces and cook 2-3 min. Correct seasoning and serve. Stew should be moist but not liquid.

Variation: When made in the summer it is typical to stir in pieces of fresh peaches.

Carbonada - a wholesome and filling stew.

The Desserts

Ambrosia

A number of desserts use this name. This recipe is one of the simplest and tastiest.

Ingredients: **1 generous tablespoon cornstarch - 2 cups sugar - 1-1/2 cups boiling water - 1 beaten egg plus 2 egg yolks - 4 tablespoons fresh strained orange juice - pinch of nutmeg.**

Method: Mix cornstarch and sugar in a small pan. Add boiling water. Stir over medium flame until mixture boils. Cook over low flame for 3 min. Beat together the eggs, juice and a pinch of nutmeg. Remove cornstarch from heat and pour in the orange mixture. Return to heat and simmer for 2 min.

Serve chilled in stemmed glasses with a sprinkling of chopped nuts on top (optional)

Apple Pan Cake

This dessert is unique to Argentina, prepared in this manner.
Ingredients: **Butter - sugar - pancake batter - peeled, cored and thinly sliced apples**

Method: Generously melt butter in a clean frying pan. Sprinkle generously with sugar. Place on high heat and when the mixture begins to bubble pour in a thin layer of batter. Cover with apple slices and cook until sugar begins to caramelise. Now adopt one of two methods: Prepare a second frying pan with a sugar caramel already prepared and flip the pancake, clean side down onto it. Cook a minute more and serve on a hot plate, OR sprinkle ample sugar onto upper side of pancake and slide onto a hot serving plate. Place plate under a hot grill until sugar melts. Serve as hot as possible.

WINE QUALITY

The reader will note that there has been no mention in the bodega profiles about the flavor of their various wines - this is deliberate. For a very long period of time the publishers of this book have conducted wine education classes on almost every continent. The one thing that we are sure of is that the perception and enjoyment of wine, whether it be subjective or objective, is very personal and individual.

During these classes we regularly give students smell-tests with common flavors and the results are not only extraordinary, but they are driven by different cultures. Wine writers like to describe many red wines as having cherry or blackberry flavors, yet, surprisingly, only one person in over 30,000 students has ever identified the smell of cherry - and not one has ever chosen the aroma of blackberries.

The following are some of the strange things students have perceived in very common kitchen foods starting with the aroma of strawberries which has been called: *peach, cherry, vanilla, musk, cough medicine, apple juice, jelly beans, rose perfume, chewing gum, caramel, chocolate, mango, pineapple, apricot.*

Ginger has been called: *soap, three-in-one oil, turpentine, pine-gum, grass, gasoline, onion, rancid butter, lemon, citronella, moth balls, cedar, oil of cloves.*

Apricot has been called: *hard candy, mango, pineapple, Hawaiian punch, peppermint, strawberry, shampoo, orange, gingerbread.*

So often we talk about quality, but what is quality? The psychological aspect of quality rests in anticipation and expectation.

We preset standards for almost any activity in which we participate; if the event or product lives up to our expectations it's fairly sure that we will give it top quality rating.

Professor Ann C. Noble of the University of California enology school, has this to say: *Since quality is a composite response to the sensory properties of the wine, based on our expectations which have been developed from our previous experiences with a wide range of wines and our own personal preferences, this judgement is an individual response. No two people integrate the individual attributes in the same way, much less have the same preferences.* Remember, this last sentence and you will enjoy wine!

All wine evaluation is about a search for quality. It is an attempt to negotiate the disputed territory between objective standards and personal preferences.

We don't judge our favorite jug red in the same category as we judge a great Argentine Malbec any more than we would judge a Jeep in terms of a Rolls Royce, although both may be recognized as quality products. They're aimed at different social occasions, different people and different prices!

Our expectations have begun to define our concept of quality by setting up relevant categories of judgment. Cost may well be a factor here. Within such general categories, further expectations are set up by our own experience. Allowances may be made for brilliant intuition, but on the whole the greater our range of experience - in wine, as in art or music or literature - the better our judgment, and the more authoritative our sense of quality is likely to be.

Anticipation plays a part in enjoyment and appreciation of all human activity from sex to fishing — or the enjoyment of music. Anticipation can be misleading as seen by the hordes of 'label-drinkers' - but, if properly developed, it can be a positive factor in determining wine quality.

Wine *flavor* comes essentially from three areas: - the weather/climate, the vineyard and the winery.

The weather will dictate the chemical composition of the fruit, and provide fully mature, ripe grapes. Good vineyard management will maximize the above. The winery will determine wine styles such as sparkling or still wines and the many other nuances.

For more on this subject we recommend **Making Sense of Wine -** *A Study in Sensory Evaluation*, available from the publisher of this book.

Wine judges in the elusive search for quality

BIBLIOGRAPHY

MENDOZA - A Land of Sun and Wine
Fernando Vidal Buzzi - Augusto Foix   1994   Foix Freres S.A. Publishers

LOS VITIVINICULTORES MENDOCINO Y SU MAGIA
Rodolfo Reina Rutini   1993   Bodegas La Rural

WINE IS FUN - textbook for the IWA Cellar Masters Diploma
Alan Young   1996   International Wine Academy

PHOTO CREDITS

152

FURTHER READING

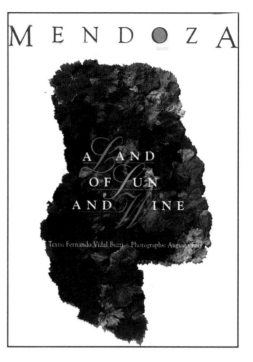

MENDOZA

A LAND OF SUN & WINE

The ultimate book for Mendoza winelovers

A monthly magazine for food and winelovers

GLOSSARY

Acetic Bacteria: Turns alcohol into water and acetic acid. Vinegar is a form of acetic acid.

Acidity: Tartness; the sharp taste of natural grape acid. Contributes to the flavor and keeping qualities. Not to be confused with sourness.

Acescence: Referring to sour taste, possibly from acetic acid.

After-Flavor: The flavor remaining in the mouth and nose.

Ampelography: Study of grapes.

Aroma: The smell of the wine from the grape, whether distinctly varietal or merely vinous, as opposed to *bouquet* coming from maturation in the bottle.

Aromatic: Fragrant, a richness of aroma and flavor, from aromatic grape varieties like Muscat, Riesling, Traminer.

Astringent: A dry, mouth-puckering effect caused by a high tannin content. May soften as the wine matures.

Aperitif: Wine taken before meals to stimulate the appetite.

Auslese: (ows-lay-zeh): German term for white wine made from selected bunches

Austere: A tough and severe wine; simple, lacking in complexity.

Baked: A *hot* and cooked smell produced by burnt and shrivelled grapes due to excessive sunshine.

Balance: The combination and relationship of component parts.

Baume: Used in Australia and Portugal as a measure of sugar in grape juice or wine. One degree of baume equals 1.8 percentage of sugar. Brix is another measure of sugar.

Big: A wine full of flavor and high in alcohol, tannin, acidity and extract.

Bitter: A *taste* term; registers at the back of the mouth.

Body: The weight of wine in the mouth due to its alcoholic content, extract and other physical components.

Bodega: A wine cellar (Spanish).

Bouquet: The part of the **nose** which comes from the fermentation and ageing processes - with *aroma,* makes up the *nose*.

Brix: (Bricks) or Balling. A hydrometer calibrated measure of sugar used mainly in the USA and NZ.

Brut: Drier type of champagne.

Capsule: Covering for top of bottle - made from plastic, foil or wax - to protect against leaking, borers and refilling. Improves appearance of bottle.

Caramel: A slightly burnt, toffee-like flavor.

Carbon Dioxide: Responsible for the bubbles in sparkling wines and the tingle of *spritzig* or effervescent table wines.

Character: *Smell* and *flavor* term - referring to vinosity and style.

Clean: Wine free of off-flavors or tastes.

Clone: A sub-variety or strain that has developed within a particular grape variety.

Cloudy: Suspended matter in solution, obscuring its clarity and color.

Cloying: A sweet and heavy wine lacking the acidity to make it crisp and interesting.

Coarse: Rough texture; lacking style and poor fruit or processing.

Corky: A distinct earthy smell of cork, arising from bacteria in the cork.

Crisp: Usually refers to white wines of good acidity that stimulate the taste senses. Normally a characteristic of grapes grown in cool climates.

Dessert Wine: Those taken at the end of a meal, e.g. port, liqueur muscat or the sweeter sherry styles.

Developed: A maturity stage, balanced, rounded, at its best.

Dry: Opposite to sweet - not wet - without sugar.

Dull: 1. Appearance - not bright; 2. nose and in-mouth lacking interest.

Dumb: Undeveloped but with inherent promise of quality. Often the sign of an *adolescent* stage.

Earthy: Characteristic smell and flavor derived from certain soils containing the chemical geosmin.

Enology: U.S. spelling of oenology.

154

Elevage: Literally *raising* ; describes the operations of maturing and blending young wines to attain better balance and quality.

Estate-Bottled: Bottled at the winery adjoining the vineyards where the grapes were grown. Local interpretations have broadened this original meaning.

Ethyl Alcohol: The purest alcohol - not poisonous to the human system. A product of fermented grape juice.

Fat: Full body, high in glycerol and extract.

Fermentation: The miracle of turning grape juice to wine. Yeast enzymes convert grape sugars to ethyl alcohol and carbon dioxide.

Fermentation, *alcoholic*: Transformation of the sugar contained in the must, into alcohol and carbon dioxide, in the presence of yeasts.

Fermentation, *malolactic*: Follows the alcoholic fermentation. Malic acid is affected by specific bacteria and changed into lactic acid and carbon dioxide. Because lactic acid is less harsh than malic acid, when young the wine becomes softer and more pleasant to drink.

Filtering: Process of separation of unwanted elements such as lees or dead yeast from the wine.

Fining: Way of clearing wines before they are bottled. With this method a colloid is added to the wine to absorb suspended particles and to fall with gravity to the bottom of the container. Products used are beaten egg white, fish glue, casein or bentonite, a type of clay. The wine is then drawn off and usually filtered before bottling.

Finish: Last impression left in the mouth by the wine.

Firm: Positive in the mouth.

Flabby: Too much fruit, too little acid and usually coarse.

Flat: Sparkling wine that has lost its *bubbles* - or a dull and uninteresting still wine usually lacking acid.

Flowery: Pleasantly aromatic - in young white wines with freshness.

Fortified: Refers to wines with added grape spirit, e.g. port, sherry, marsala.

Fruity: Aroma and flavor of fresh grapes or other fruits.

Free Run Wine: Unpressed wine drawn off during or after fermentation**.**

Generic: Wine names which refer to historic or geographic areas, e.g. burgundy, moselle, sherry, port.

Green: Common to *taste* and *smell* - excessive grape acid - sharp flavor.

Grip: A firm combination of physical characteristics, mainly tannin.

Hard: Dry, almost bitter, unpleasant, too much acid and/or tannin.

Heady: Wines high in alcohol.

Hectare: One hundred square metres, the equivalent of 2.47 acres.

Hedonistic: A simple subjective, personal rating, eg pleasant to the individual taster.

Late Picked: Wine made from grapes left longer on vines to reach high sugar levels - see Spatlese.

Lees: Made up of latent yeasts, tartars and residual matter from the fruit. The lees form a dark yellow deposit at the bottom of the cask. These are removed during racking.

Light: A confusing term that can apply to the alcoholic strength of a wine. A full-bodied wine can be *light* on flavor.

Limpid: Clear (appearance).

Long: Lingering flavor; a sign of quality.

Magnum: A large bottle with a capacity of 1.5 litres or the equivalent of two ordinary bottles. Fine wines are more slowly aged in magnums than in 75 ml bottles.

Malic Acid: An acid from grapes and green apples which leaves a puckering sensation in the mouth.

Marc: The residue of skins and seeds after juice is extracted by pressing.

Mellow: Soft, mature, evolved and ripe.

Mouldy: An undesirable flavor imparted by rotten grapes or stale, unclean, casks etc.

Must: Crushed grapes or juice until the end of fermentation, then becomes wine.

Negociant: The person who buys wine from the grower and sells it to wholesalers.

Neutral: Without positive flavor or marked characteristics. A common feature of many poorly blended wines.

Nose: The combined *bouquet* and *aroma* of wine.

NV: (non vintage). For ports, champagnes or other wines.

Oaky: Flavor obtained by ageing wine in new oak casks.

O/Enology: The science of wine and winemaking.

Olfactory: The sense of smell and its perception.

Organoleptic: Using the senses of sight, smell, touch and taste to evaluate food and wine.

Oxidation: Change in wine caused by exposure to air. Can have beneficial effects, but over-exposure brings about discoloration and loss of flavor.

Pricked: An unpleasant sharpness due to excess volatile acidity.

Puckering : A tactile sensation usually caused by high tannin content.

Pungent: Highly aromatic and earthy smell.

Racking: Separating wine from its *lees* by transferring from one container to another.

Rancio: A *smell* term associated with aged and oxidized sherries, usually denoting high quality.

Residual Sugar: Normally in white wine where fermentation has been stopped to allow some natural grape sugar to remain.

Round: A wine harmoniously balanced, in body and flavor.

Sec: French for dry - seco in Spanish and Portuguese.

Sekt: German for sparkling wine.

Soft: A wine low in alcohol.

Solera: System of progressive blending of young and old wines in tiers of small casks. A Spanish development for maturation of sherry - used in other countries in modified form for both sherry and port.

Sour: Disagreeably acid, acetic acid - vinegary.

Spatlese: (schpate-lay-zuh) German term for a wine category made from grapes picked late in the season to make mostly sweet white table wine.

Spicy: Wines of pronounced varietal character, muscat and traminer are good examples.

Spumante: Italian for sparkling or frothy wine.

Sulfury (Sulphury): Generally refers to sulfur (sulphur) dioxide - the most common antiseptic in wine making.

Supple: Mouth-filling, easy to drink.

Tactile: The *touch* sense.

Tannin: A natural substance in grape skins, seeds and oak casks. Provides the "backbone" in red wine.

Tart: Possessing agreeable high acidity from the natural fruit acid.

Tawny: Wines with red to brownish color. Applies to ports and red wines.

Threshold: Level at which a given smell or taste can be perceived. Thresholds vary from person to person, from substance to substance.

Thin: Lack of body, watery.

Tinto: Red.

Ullage: The space between the wine and the cork, or wine and cask.

Varietal: Wine made from a single grape variety.

Vendange Tardives: Late harvesting, mainly in Alsatian wines.

Veraison: When the fruit changes color during ripening.

Viniculture - grape production for winemaking.

Vinosity: Having positive, wine character.

Viticulture: The study and practice of grape production.

Vignoble: Wine growing area.

Vigneron: Winegrower.

Vintage: Harvesting of grapes and converting grapes to wine.

Vintner: Wine merchant.

Vinosity: A tasting term relating to grape character and alcoholic strength of wine.

INDEX

157